ROADSIDE GUIDE TO

Indian Ruins

& Rock Art

OF THE SOUTHWEST

TEXT & PHOTOGRAPHY BY

Gordon and Cathie Sullivan

WESTCLIFFE PUBLISHERS

westcliffepublishers.com

For more information about other fine books and calendars from Westcliffe Publishers, please contact your local bookstore, call us at 1-800-523-3692, or visit us on the Web at westcliffepublishers.com.

INTERNATIONAL STANDARD BOOK NUMBERS:
ISBN-10: 1-56579-481-8
ISBN-13: 978-1-56579-481-8

TEXT AND PHOTOGRAPHY COPYRIGHT:
Gordon and Cathie Sullivan, 2005. All rights reserved.

EDITOR: Elizabeth Train
DESIGNER: Rebecca Finkel, F + P Graphic Design, Inc.
PRODUCTION MANAGER: Craig Keyzer

PUBLISHED BY:
Westcliffe Publishers, Inc.
P.O. Box 1261
Englewood, CO 80150
westcliffepublishers.com

Printed in China by Hing Yip Printing Co., Ltd.

LIBRARY OF CONGRESS CATALOGING-IN-PUBLICATION DATA:
Sullivan, Gordon.
   Roadside guide to Indian ruins & rock art of the Southwest / text & photography by Gordon & Cathie Sullivan.
      p. cm.
   Includes index.
   ISBN-13: 978-1-56579-481-8
   ISBN-10: 1-56579-481-8
   1. Indians of North America—Southwest, New—Antiquities—Guidebooks. 2. Petroglyphs—Southwest, New—Guidebooks. 3. Southwest, New—Antiquities—Guidebooks. I. Sullivan, Cathie. II. Title.
   E78.S7S93 2005
   709'.01'130979—dc22

                                                    2004028659

COVER PHOTO:
Hovenweep National Monument, Utah

BACK COVER PHOTO:
Painted Rocks State Park, Arizona

1ST FRONTISPIECE:
Lomaki Pueblo, Wupatki National Monument, Arizona

2ND FRONTISPIECE:
Great Kiva, Lowry Pueblo, Canyon of the Ancients National Monument, Colorado

TITLE PAGE:
Petroglyph, Monument Valley, Arizona

PLEASE NOTE: Risk is always a factor in backcountry and high-mountain travel. Many of the activities described in this book can be dangerous, especially when weather is adverse or unpredictable, and when unforeseen events or conditions create a hazardous situation. The authors have done their best to provide the reader with accurate information about backcountry travel, as well as to point out some of its potential hazards. It is the responsibility of the users of this guide to learn the necessary skills for safe backcountry travel, and to exercise caution in potentially hazardous areas. The author and publisher disclaim any liability or injury or other damage caused by backcountry traveling or performing any other activity described in this book.

Opposite: Raingod Mesa, Monument Valley National Monument, Arizona

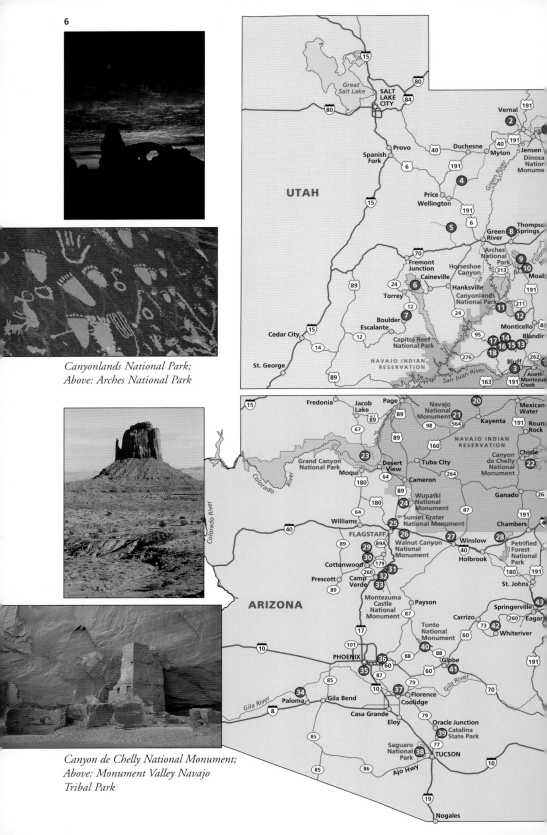

Canyonlands National Park;
Above: Arches National Park

Canyon de Chelly National Monument;
Above: Monument Valley Navajo
Tribal Park

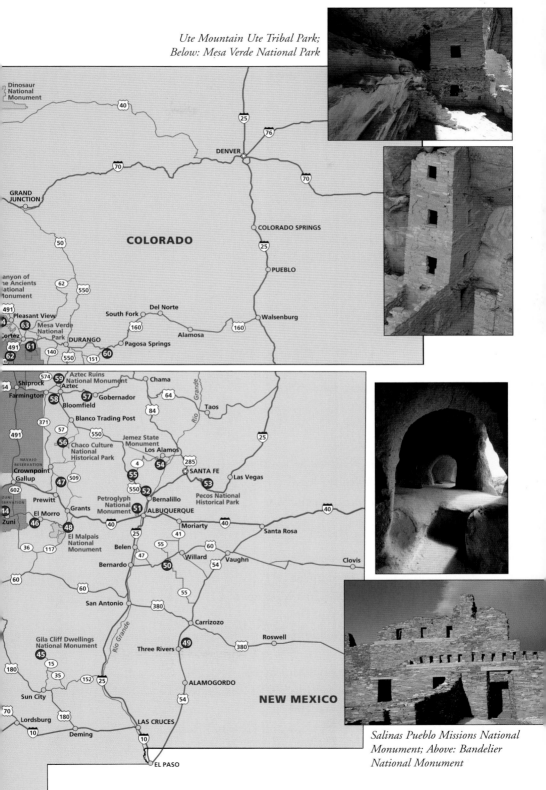

Ute Mountain Ute Tribal Park;
Below: Mesa Verde National Park

Dinosaur National Monument

40

25

76

DENVER

70

70

GRAND JUNCTION

COLORADO SPRINGS

50

COLORADO

25

PUEBLO

anyon of ne Ancients ational Monument

62

550

Del Norte

South Fork

160

Walsenburg

491

Pleasant View

63

Mesa Verde National Park

160

Alamosa

ortez

DURANGO

Pagosa Springs

491

61

140

550

151

60

62

574

59

Aztec Ruins National Monument

Chama

Shiprock

Aztec

57

Gobernador

64

Farmington

58

Bloomfield

Taos

84

371

Blanco Trading Post

491

57

56

550

Jemez State Monument

25

Chaco Culture National Historical Park

Los Alamos

NAVAJO RESERVATION

4

54

285

Crownpoint

55

SANTA FE

Gallup

47

509

53

Las Vegas

602

550

52

ZUNI SERVATION

Prewitt

Petroglyph National Monument

Bernalillo

Pecos National Historical Park

14

Grants

51

ALBUQUERQUE

Zuni

46

48

40

40

El Morro

El Malpais National Monument

40

Moriarty

Santa Rosa

36

117

25

41

Belen

55

60

47

Willard

54

Vaughn

Clovis

Bernardo

50

60

55

60

San Antonio

380

Gila Cliff Dwellings National Monument

Rio Grande

Carrizozo

45

Three Rivers

49

Roswell

380

180

15

35

152

25

Sun City

ALAMOGORDO

70

54

NEW MEXICO

Lordsburg

180

LAS CRUCES

10

Deming

10

EL PASO

Salinas Pueblo Missions National Monument; Above: Bandelier National Monument

Contents

Preface

My work as a nature photographer first brought me to the Four Corners region almost three decades ago. Coming from a high-mountain home in Montana, I was completely unprepared as an imagemaker for the vast desert landscape with its deep, shadowed canyons, flattop mesas, and diverse life zones. My creative eyes were accustomed to cascading waterfalls, snow-covered peaks, and lush, green meadows—all scenes indigenous to the North Country. I was used to treading over landscapes virtually pulsating from the effects of abundant, free-flowing water and the thriving ecosystems ample water creates. When I first arrived in the desert land, I felt as if I were stepping onto an unsettled moonscape—an outlandish corner of a faraway universe, light years from the familiar places where I had grown as an outdoor photographer.

Each time the red dust of the Southwest rose in dry clouds around my shuffling feet, I was reminded of how much I had to learn about this strange environment before my photographs could become meaningful. The vast, semi-arid vistas, weathered earth, and bone-dry plains, oftentimes set before lofty mountains, demanded what grew to become a spiritual connection to the landscape for me. My reverence for the red desert evolved into a connection often reserved for those who are born in an area, grow up in its midst, and are intimately familiar with its moods and seasons. And, after several visits to the Southwest, I truly felt a kinship with this land.

Aside from its physical difference from other places that I had worked, there was something else unusual about the desert landscape. I was keenly aware of the haunting human history that threads itself through the very fabric of the Southwest. Distant voices seemed to call out from the sacred ruins, seeking the willing ear of those endeavoring to understand the ancient people who once inhabited this land—a people who constructed stone hamlets the size of small, modern cities and marked their passage by etching and painting artful designs deep into the sandstone cliffs; a people who mysteriously vanished from their villages like clouds of red dust rising from the desert floor, leaving beautiful stone structures and rock-art displays as testaments to their presence here. It was the muffled cries of the ancient ones, resounding like a distant drumbeat from the parched earth, that finally hooked me as an artist to the wonders of the Southwest.

To even the casual observer, the Southwest is composed of two inextricable features. The first looms before us in the breathtaking natural landscape, full of sandstone sculptures carved by time. The geologic splendor of these lands couples with the lingering presence of prehistoric human life—a presence so much a part of the physical environment it acts as the very soul of the land. To artistically

Pueblo del Arroyo, Chaco Culture National Historical Park, New Mexico

portray one element without the other would be impossible. From the onset, I realized it would take decades of experience for me to successfully blend the two faces of the desert into a single image—to finally expose the subtle grace that lay hidden within these vast spaces and among the echoing voices of the land.

It was this quest for a creative connection that kept me coming back. However, it wasn't until I met my life's partner, Cathie, that I started to see things through the glass eye of my camera in a different way. She was a portrait photographer and had practiced her art for more than 25 years. She had honed her creative eye to judge the value of a successful photograph more by the human faces pictured within than the light falling on rock and water. She clearly saw the human side of the natural world that I so often missed, and she saw, in full exposure, the human face of the Southwest.

Our Southwest journey was spawned one evening as we sat together high atop the sandstone walls overlooking the ruins at New Mexico's Chaco Canyon. It was mid November, and we had arrived in the canyon late in the afternoon, with just enough time to hike the steep trail that leads to the canyon's upper ridge. We rested on a flat sandstone boulder and watched the western sun melt like butter over the distant horizon—the final act of a timeless drama performed to perfection each day in this primal place. Like a closing curtain, the dense black shadow of night inched its way along the canyon floor, following the gradual sinking of the setting sun. As the western sky drained itself of hue and gradually filled with stars, we sat above the ancient place and planned the next four years of our life as photographers, dedicating our time and energy to capturing the cultural and natural landscapes of the Southwest.

That night was the beginning of a wonderful learning experience for Cathie and me as we followed the route of the first people across the rugged landscape. Our years of travel took us thousands of miles through countless dark canyons and down an endless ribbon of paved and gravel roads. They also sent our eyes across the printed pages of numerous books, reports, manuscripts, and archaeological studies, enlightening and educating us about the people who once lived in this magical place. And, of course, they consumed *lots and lots* of film. We chose the images in this book from a collection of more than 6,500 photographs taken on our four-year journey—a journey that we feel helped us grow a great deal as artists. For, as our work progressed, the connection between the natural environment and its cultural past became more and more vivid in our photographs. We feel that our portrayal of this inextricable relationship between the land and its past improved by leaps and bounds, exposing the very soul of the Southwest. We hope you agree!

With the help of Westcliffe Publishers, we offer you our photographic view in *Roadside Guide to Indian Ruins & Rock Art of the Southwest.* We are grateful to the dedicated people at Westcliffe for giving life to our images and text through the pages of this guidebook. We thank all those who lent us a hand along the way and helped us to understand more about the ancient cultures of the Southwest as well as our own past as humans on this earth. We especially thank the many Native American people who welcomed us into their world and provided us with valuable insight into their ancestral past.

Above all else, we thank the powerful influences of places like Chaco Canyon, where people who take the time to listen and to learn can begin to understand the oneness of people, past and present. We are all fellow travelers, explorers, and adventurers in this world. From the darkened sandstone cliffs far above the magnificent canyons to your tabletop, we offer our inspired view of the natural and human faces of the Southwest.

Three Rivers Petroglyph Site, New Mexico;
Left: Buckhorn Wash Rock Art, Utah

History of the Four Corners Region

Thousands of years before the first Europeans arrived in the American Southwest, native people made their homes here. Their ancient villages spread across the red-rock landscape, and their crops thrived in the canyon bottoms and rich floodplains. The rock art, pottery shards, and crumbling buildings they left behind tell some of the story of the area's first inhabitants, but many questions remain. Where did the original people of the Southwest come from? How did they arrive? The answers trace back to another continent—a place far north of the red-rock deserts, in a land we now know as Siberia—and to a time that is nearly inconceivable.

Navajo basket, Arizona

After hundreds of years of study, a growing group of scholars now supports the theory that the indigenous people who spread across the North American continent were descendants of the Mongoloid race who arrived here from Asia. Their unhurried migration to the New World began as far back as 36,000 to 12,000 years ago. The people are thought to have crossed the Beringia land bridge, now a shallow section of the Bering Sea located between the eastern coast of Siberia and the western coast of Alaska, which was exposed when the ocean levels fell during the last ice age.

These ancient pioneers were nomadic hunters and probably made their way through the vastness of the New World in pursuit of wandering herds of mastodons, prehistoric camels, and furry bison. Because of their nomadic way of life and the constant need to follow the herds, these early people never settled in one place for very long. Instead, they lived in crudely constructed brush houses and often dwelled in caves or beneath cliff overhangs. As a result, few substantial traces were left behind to mark their presence.

However, one thing is known for sure. The hunters and gatherers, by sheer necessity, were well adapted to the diverse environments in which they lived.

They carried tools and weapons made of stone, including large knives, heavy hammers, and sharp spearheads. Archaeologists call these ancient weapons Clovis, named after the spot in present-day New Mexico where some of the spear points were first discovered. Clovis points and piles of bones left at hunting and butchering sites are some of the only remains that enable archaeologists to date these early civilizations. The Clovis points found in the Southwest probably date back to sometime between 9500 B.C. and 8500 B.C.

These nomads from the Arctic followed the gradual movements of wild game as the herds headed southward, searching for grazing grounds along ice-free corridors. The people crossed the wilds we know today as Alaska, the Northwest Territories, and western Canada, finally entering the northern border of what was to become the United States. Somewhere in the Northwest Territories the migratory paths split. One group headed down the West Coast, finally reaching the tip of the Baja Peninsula. A second group drifted toward the area of the Great

Lakes and eventually inhabited lands all along the East Coast and farther into the Southeast. The third group, the ancestors of the ancient people of the American Southwest, crossed the Great Plains, the Great Basin, and then entered the red desert region.

As they followed game trails among washes and canyon bottoms, the wanderers gathered wild plants and lived in temporary structures like wooden

Navajo pottery, Arizona

lean-tos and makeshift pithouses. For some of these nomads, the southward drifting ended in the deserts here, and they allowed their roots to grow deep in the desert sands. As generations went by these people learned to cultivate crops, and they gradually evolved from hunting and gathering to an agriculturally based society.

Their dwellings reflected this cultural change by becoming more permanent and community oriented. Impressive pueblos and cliff dwellings housed hundreds of people in self-contained farming villages, complete with storage rooms for the harvest and ceremonial kivas to honor the people's spiritual connection to the earth. Today, many of these structures remain standing, at least in part and serve as testaments to the architectural ingenuity and skill of the early people.

As you visit the sites in this book, it is important to remember that they are sacred places. While walking among the ancient ruins and rock-art sites of the Anasazi, Mogollon, Hohokam, Sinagua, and Salado, you are weaving your way through the ancestral lands of the Pueblo, Hopi, Zuni, Navajo, Apache, and Ute people. You will find a vibrant connection between today's native people and the ancient ones of the Southwest—a connection that is best understood by visiting the present-day tribes and taking advantage of their growing desire to educate the public about native people, past and present. Their marvelous oral tradition connects modern Indians to ancient ones and provides valuable clues to the mysteries left unsolved by science.

Opposite: Horsecollar Ruins, Natural Bridges National Monument, Utah

How to Use this Guide

There are thousands of prehistoric sites scattered throughout the Four Corners region, which encompasses Utah, Arizona, New Mexico, and Colorado. Some of these sites are under the management of federal and state agencies, some are under the stewardship of Native American tribes, and still others lie in remote and unprotected places, awaiting discovery. The images and words in this guidebook are the products of our years of travel throughout the Southwest and will lead you to the most popular and culturally significant sites in the region. We've tried to provide you with useful information and helpful hints about visiting these ancient sites—guidance we wish we'd had when we first set out to explore the Southwest, years ago!

The destinations in this book include both ruin and rock-art sites, ranging from full-service national monuments, with museums and guided tours, to pictograph panels that sit silently at the end of an unmarked road. Many of the sites lie within a short walk from a paved parking lot, while a few blossom into view after a strenuous hike. Some are close to the outskirts of major cities, and others are more remote, requiring a scenic drive through spectacular country to reach them. This book will help you find the most accessible points of ancestral interest as well as places to seek solitude among the ancient ruins.

We have provided quick facts at the beginning of each entry for contact information, hours of operation, and fees when applicable. A list of websites appears on p. 232. We've also tried to give you a sense of the level of interpretation and educational opportunities (or lack thereof) available at each site, so you'll know what to expect before you arrive and can call for information or make reservations accordingly. Because of their cultural and archaeological importance, a number of sites have been placed under the protection of the federal government or are carefully managed by native tribes. General access to these sites may be limited, so call ahead for current information before you head to these unique areas.

> The more we traveled through the Southwest, the more we learned how to do so efficiently. We found that linking a number of sites enabled us to maximize our time in each area, and we've shared some of our favorite road-trip loops in the appendix (p. 221).

We also provide general directions to each site, as well as maps that show their location, but we encourage you to purchase a good set of detailed maps before heading out on your adventure. We recommend the "Recreation Maps" for each of the Four Corners states, published by GTR Mapping. Available where books and maps are sold, they provide a nice degree of detail, including mileages and road numbers in remote areas. It might also be helpful to have an atlas or city map for navigating urban areas.

Opposite: Bandelier National Monument, New Mexico

After the nitty-gritty information, we offer a short description to help give you an overview of the cultural significance of each site. We've made a particular effort to portray the human side of these sites, both through our images and in our text. After all, it was our interest in the people who once lived in the Southwest that really fueled our explorations here and kept us coming back to the red-rock country again and again.

Cathie and I are not archaeologists or anthropologists; we are photographers, first and foremost. However, during the time we traveled and worked in this area, we managed to learn a great deal about the people and cultural landscapes. So much of what is known about the first people of the desert—their lifestyle, customs, art, and architecture—is still a mystery to experts, which makes discussions beyond certain levels a matter of conjecture at best. We hope our musings will be helpful as you begin your own quest to understand the ancient people of the Southwest. Allow our impressions to be your starting point and to fuel your sense of personal discovery.

Leave Only Footprints

Though they've stood the test of time, the ruins and rock-art sites in the Southwest are very fragile, and human impact on these special places can be devastating. In fact, most archaeological sites have received more destructive damage within the last hundred years from human hands than they experienced during all of the previous centuries of weathering and erosion combined. Though many sites featured in this book are protected by the dedicated work of the National Park Service, the BLM, or private owners, it remains up to all of us who visit these archaeological treasures to help in their preservation efforts. Here are some things to keep in mind when exploring ruins and rock-art sites:

- **Stay on designated paths and trails when touring sites.**
  Most of the sites in this book are managed by the park service or state agencies, and established trails help manage visitors. Breaking new trails can negatively impact plants and wildlife and disturb the archaeological work being done in the area. Some of the more remote sites do not have established trails, and it is your responsibility to tread lightly through these fragile areas. (For more information on low-impact backcountry travel, visit the Leave No Trace website at lnt.org.)

- **Respect the rules at each site.**
  Some sites, particularly those that are culturally or archaeologically sensitive, have specific rules that must be followed in order to preserve sacred places or scientific studies. Please honor the wishes of the stewards who manage each site.

- **Do not touch structures, artifacts, or rock art.**
  Touching a petroglyph or pictograph will result in permanent damage and will drastically shorten the life of the image. Please observe ruins and rock art from a distance, and leave nothing behind but your footprints in the desert sand.

- **Never remove artifacts from ANY site, no matter how remote.**
  Though this goes without saying, it's an important point! Artifacts belong to the areas where they are found and have no place in pockets or personal display cases.

Opposite: Pueblo interior, Pueblo Grande Museum and Archaeological Park, Arizona

Introduction

The Southwest is a landscape rich with prehistoric and historic traces. This guidebook is designed to serve as both your map and an initial introduction to the prehistoric ruins and rock art of this unique area. The depth of your exploration is up to you and can range from a day spent at one site to a week or two of traveling in the red-rock country. Regardless of its length, your journey through the land of the ancient ones will remain with you long after you've left the canyons, timbered mountains, and wide, sweeping mesas here.

The area we've covered in this book spans the southwestern corner of Colorado, the southeastern reaches of Utah, and the states of New Mexico and Arizona and includes all the major indigenous cultures of the region as well as many of the subcultures that resulted from the continued habitation of the original people. The sites included in this book were selected to provide a diverse sampling of the dwellings, campsites, and rock art of these prehistoric people—ancient ancestors of the Native Americans who still inhabit the Southwest today—and to illuminate the important cultural contributions these people made to the growth of our present society.

Examples of this human progress are particularly evident at sites that span not only generations but entire cultures. For example, the remote reaches of Sego Canyon in southeastern Utah bear the artwork of contemporary Ute artisans alongside the archaic work of nomadic visitors who paused here in their pursuit of wild game. The paintings on these stone walls record centuries of human presence and literally catalog the passage of time.

Many sites feature visitor centers, interpretive displays, and guided tours of the ruins and rock art. Sites such as the ruins at Chimney Rock can be viewed up close as their story is told by excellent guides who offer stories and facts hidden from the casual observer. But not all of the sites in this book are established tourist destinations. There are places where a visitor can sit for hours in the silence and listen to the wind sweep across the sandstone walls. These sites invite adventurers to roam the land as the original residents once did.

Hopefully, this book will perk your interest and inspire you to seek many of the incredible cultural sites the Southwest has to offer. There is a clear link between the nomads who ventured to this land thousands of years ago and the modern travelers who visit these ancient sites today. For even though we are separated by a span of unimaginable time, we are still explorers, still adventurers. We are a species compelled by the spirit and mystery of discovery.

Opposite: Canyon de Chelly National Monument, Arizona

Utah

Cedar City

St. George

Hovenweep National Monument;
Left: Natural Bridges National Monument

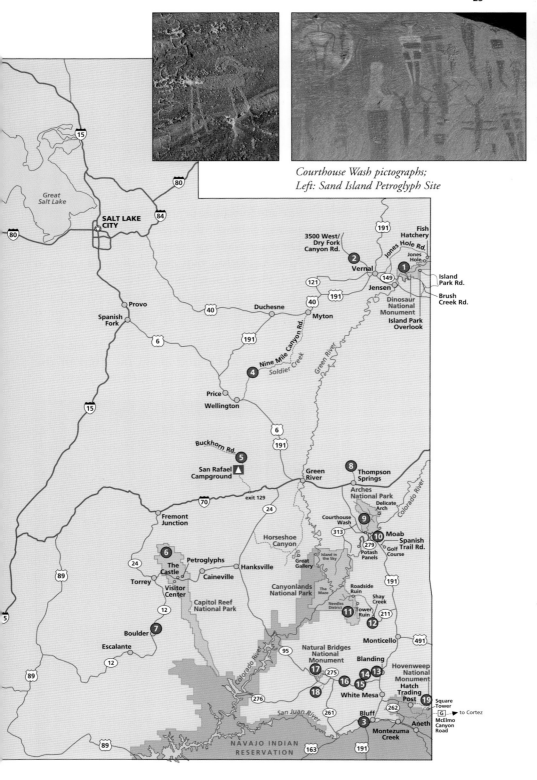

Courthouse Wash pictographs;
Left: Sand Island Petroglyph Site

1 DINOSAUR NATIONAL MONUMENT

4545 E. Highway 40
Dinosaur, CO 81610-9724
(970) 374-3000

NEAREST SUPPLY CENTER:
Vernal, Utah

HIGHLIGHTS: Dinosaur National Monument is best known for its large quarry of fossilized dinosaur remains and rugged natural setting along the Green River. However, the monument also features one of the country's best-preserved Fremont rock-art collections.

INTERPRETATION:
Visitor centers and self-guided tours

SEASONS OPEN: All seasons, but March–October are best

HOURS OF OPERATION:
Call for the visitor centers' seasonal hours

FEE AREA: Yes

ACCESS ROAD: Paved

DIRECTIONS: Dinosaur National Monument spans both Utah and Colorado. The entrance closest to the rock-art sites is approximately 20 miles from the town of Vernal on UT 149. The Tour of the Tilted Rocks leads to the most accessible rock-art panels, and guides for this and other auto tours can be purchased at the visitor centers.

Many wonders lie within the 210,000 acres of Dinosaur National Monument. From the geological formations, to the famed remains of dinosaurs, to the rock art left behind by many generations of Fremont artisans, the area is laced with relics from the distant past. Contemporary Ute and Shoshone people believe their ancestors passed through the area around Vernal and Dinosaur National Monument during the spiritual migration that eventually lead them to their present homelands in Wyoming and Idaho. As a result, both of these tribes consider the rock-art sites scattered throughout the region to be sacred.

Some of the best and most accessible rock-art panels are found along the **Tour of the Tilted Rocks.** This auto tour takes about two

hours to complete and leads to some remarkable sites featuring vivid examples of classic Vernal-style Fremont rock art. The first site along this tour, called Swelter Shelter, provides a close-up view of petroglyphs believed to have been placed on the walls roughly 1,000 years ago. Legend has it that as archaeologists excavated the ancient shelter here the summer's heat became so intense the workers began to swelter—hence the name. The site probably served as a temporary campsite while Fremont hunters roamed the area in search of wild game. Petroglyphs of human and animal images blend with an assortment of geometric markings and trapezoidal figures.

You will spot a number of large lizard petroglyphs lounging on the flat surface of the overhang above the road at marker 14. Numerous images lie on the exposed surfaces around the lizards, so be sure to get a close look. A hiking trail leads from the edge of the pullout up to this amazing group of images.

Though the auto tour is a great way to see a number of impressive examples of Fremont rock art, some of the most interesting sites in the park lie off the beaten path. They are well worth hiking to, if solitude and physical exercise fit into your travel plans.

The **McKee Springs** petroglyphs are on the Island Park Road. Travel north from Jensen on UT 149 to Brush Creek Road. Turn left onto Brush Creek Road, proceed to Island Park Road, turn right, and continue for four miles until the road splits. Bear right at the fork and proceed for another 11 miles. When the road begins to narrow, look for a vivid petroglyph panel on the right.

The **Deluge Shelter** petroglyph site is near the Fish Hatchery on Jones Hole Creek. From Vernal, take Jones Hole Road to the hatchery and trailhead. A well-marked

Swelter Shelter petroglyphs

trail departs from the hatchery and follows the creek for 1.75 miles to the first interpretative sign.

It is a good idea to stop at the Vernal Chamber of Commerce to ask for specific directions and a good map to help guide you to these remote sites. You can also learn more about viewing rock art from a raft while floating down the Yampa and Green Rivers. Just remember, visitors to Dinosaur National Monument are fortunate to view prehistoric art at such close range. This opportunity comes with an equal amount of responsibility to respect and protect the beautiful rock art here.

Cub Creek petroglyphs

2 DRY FORK CANYON ROCK-ART SITE

10050 N. Dry Fork Canyon
Vernal, UT 84078
(435) 789-6733

NEAREST SUPPLY CENTER:
Vernal, Utah

HIGHLIGHTS: This fascinating
site contains some of the
clearest and best-preserved
examples of Fremont rock
art in the Southwest.

INTERPRETATION:
Self-guided tour and
informative brochures

SEASONS OPEN: All seasons

HOURS OF OPERATION:
All hours

FEE AREA:
Donations are requested

ACCESS ROAD: Paved

DIRECTIONS: The rock-art
site at Dry Fork Canyon is
10 miles northwest of the
town of Vernal. The site is
on the McConkie Ranch and
is well known in the local
community. From Main Street
in Vernal, travel north on
500 West until it intersects
with UT 121, and make a
right turn onto 3500 West
(Dry Fork Canyon Road).
Proceed north for a few miles
to a sign reading "Indian
Petroglyphs," turn left at
the sign, and proceed about
a half-mile to the parking
lot and picnic area at the
site. The last stretch is on
a dirt road.

The steep Navajo Sandstone cliffs bordering Dry Fork Canyon display an epic of erosion. However, these cliffs also bear another story. An ancient parable, etched in intricate detail, tells of the Fremont people who occupied the area from roughly A.D. 500 to 1240. The Fremont artists pecked and painted complex images onto the stone walls, giving present-day visitors to McConkie Ranch and Dry Fork Canyon a window into the past.

Dry Fork Canyon is considered by many experts to contain the largest and best-preserved collection of classic Fremont-style images to be found anywhere. Despite hundreds of years of erosion and weathering, many of the images remain startlingly clear, making this site one of the most photographed in the Southwest.

The sweeping panels contain hundreds of individual forms, including human figures and a broad display of animals.

The contemporary Shoshone and Ute people view the petroglyphs and pictographs along Dry Fork Creek as enduring, spiritual messages left by

their ancient ancestors as they migrated to their present homelands in Idaho and Wyoming. These images signify a strong and sacred connection to the land and the life it supports— a connection that is still vital to Native Americans today.

Most of the rock art at the McConkie site is accessible and easily photographed. The trail to the site begins at a small information hut at the head of the parking lot and winds its way along the lower edge of the vertical cliffs. One of the first rock-art panels along the trail bears the image of a long-bodied mountain lion that is surrounded by a number of geometric forms.

Farther down the left fork of the trail, the images begin to appear sharper and contain more complex elements in their form. Some of the largest and most detailed scenes are found toward the end of this trail, so don't exhaust your film supply too soon!

Many panels include human figures standing in line or linked by holding hands. Some of the larger figures appear to be holding circular shields, ceremonial masks, or human heads. Other panels at the site include humanoid images adorned with stylish headdresses, helmets, and, in a few cases, what appear to be horns. Many of these figures are dressed in detailed garments, complete with elaborate necklaces and ear bobs. Anthropomorphic images are also pictured either holding or standing under hoops or arches, and the figures are connected by their outstretched arms or by geometric images that they seem to be holding between them. The zoomorphic images found at the site sometimes appear in chase scenes complete with human hunters.

The rock art at Dry Fork Canyon rests on private land and is made available to the public through the goodwill of the landowners. A small and informative book compiled by Jean McConkie McKenzie titled *Rock Art* is available for purchase and discusses many of the rock-art features in the canyon. Donations, which serve as a primary source of operating capital, are welcome.

3 SAND ISLAND PETROGLYPH SITE

Bureau of Land Management
Monticello Field Office
435 N. Main St.
P.O. Box 7
Monticello, UT 84535
(435) 587-1500

NEAREST SUPPLY CENTER:
Bluff, Utah

HIGHLIGHTS: **The easily
accessed rock-art panels at
Sand Island represent the
work of Archaic, Anasazi,
Ute, and Navajo artists.**

LEVEL OF INTERPRETATION:
None

SEASONS OPEN: **All**

HOURS OF OPERATION:
All hours

FEE AREA: **No**

ACCESS ROAD: **Paved**

DIRECTIONS: **The Sand Island
Petroglyph Site is located
3 miles west of Bluff just off
US 163/191. The turnoff and
the rock-art site itself are both
well marked.**

The petroglyphs at Sand Island, like numerous other examples of rock art found in the Southwest, represent many distinct cultures. Ute, Archaic, Ancestral Puebloan (Anasazi), and Navajo art is all included on this half-mile-long panel. The early Basketmakers' anthropomorphic images, identified by trapezoidal torsos and broad shoulders, are still clearly visible, as are images attributed to the Anasazi, including deer, bighorn sheep, snakes, and other reptiles. One of the most spectacular Anasazi images at Sand Island is of Kokopelli (above), the ancient flute player. Kokopelli is both an ancestral and contemporary icon among the Native Americans of the Southwest and has inspired many legends associated with his power over human fertility.

The Ute and Navajo also left their art here, and depictions of horses and riders seem to gallop across the rocks. Hopi legend has it that several groups of ancient people arrived in this land through a single hole in the earth. Some traveled in a southerly direction and others traveled north. Some of those who headed south were light-skinned people, impatient to find a homeland. After traveling a fair distance across the desert, these white people grew sore-footed. Realizing they needed to cover a long distance in order to reach their destination, they decided to mold horses to carry them onward. This is why white people had horses long before others in the Southwest. (Although it is far less interesting, historical evidence indicates that the Spanish are responsible for bringing the first horses to the Southwest sometime after 1540.)

The well-preserved images at Sand Island rest behind a tall cyclone fence. Many of the petroglyphs are found high on the wall, and a spotting scope or a good set of binoculars might come in handy.

4 NINE MILE CANYON PETROGLYPHS

Bureau of Land Management
Price Field Office
125 South 600 West
Price, UT 84501
(435) 636-3600

NEAREST SUPPLY CENTER:
Wellington, Utah

HIGHLIGHTS: This spectacular canyon has been called "the world's largest rock-art gallery" and contains more than 10,000 images at its many sites.

LEVEL OF INTERPRETATION: Guidebooks and private tours of the area are available. Contact the BLM for more information.

SEASONS OPEN: All seasons

HOURS OF OPERATION: All hours

FEE AREA: No

ACCESS ROAD: Well-maintained gravel

DIRECTIONS: The 78-mile-long Nine Mile Canyon Road, also known as Soldier Creek Road, is just north of Wellington. The road, which is paved for the first 12 miles and turns to well-maintained gravel, heads north from US 6 and is clearly marked. It can be driven all the way to the town of Myton on US 40/191, if time allows.

It is helpful to purchase a guidebook to the rock art of Nine Mile Canyon (which can be obtained in Wellington or Myton) before heading out on your adventure. Most of the land along Nine Mile Canyon Road is private property, so a good set of binoculars or even a spotting scope might come in handy. Be sure to start the trip with a full tank of gas and plenty of drinking water. You might even consider bringing a picnic lunch to enjoy along the route. It is best to enter the canyon from the Wellington side and proceed through to Myton.

Most of the inscriptions on the rocks walls in Nine Mile Canyon (which is actually 40 miles in length) were crafted by the Fremont people, who inhabited the area between A.D. 500 and 1300. They were attracted to the area by the abundance of water, wild plants, and animals. As their agriculture progressed, the Fremont cultivated crops in the canyon's mineral-rich soil.

During their occupation here, the Fremont used the cliff faces, rock outcroppings, and large boulders to document the story of their lives. Humanoid figures swim in a sea of geometric shapes and animal renderings, including bighorn sheep, deer, and elk as well as smaller creatures like lizards and an assortment of snakes.

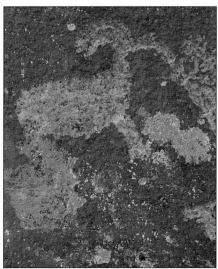

The canyon is particularly well known for its large rock-art panels depicting prehistoric hunting scenes. Cottonwood Canyon, a side canyon of Nine Mile, hosts the famous Hunting Scene Petroglyph Panel, which displays a herd of bighorn sheep heading in the direction of waiting hunters. In the middle of the herd there is a horned, trapezoidal figure of considerable size that appears to play an active role in the hunt. Some scholars believe this figure may be a shaman placed among the sheep to ensure the hunters' success. This theory supports the importance many prehistoric cultures placed on the spiritual elements surrounding their lives. Regardless of its meaning, the impressive hunting panel is worth the effort it takes to view first hand.

The small collections of ruins in the area are found, for the most part, on the high walls above the drainages. Most of the remaining buildings are granaries and storage structures. The Fremont people did not use mortar in the construction of their dwellings—a technique known today as "dry laying"—so many of the ancient walls have fallen to rubble over the years.

The rock art found along Nine Mile Canyon Road and throughout the side canyons is quite different in style from others in the area, such as Dry Fork Canyon and Dinosaur National Monument. The anthropomorphic figures here are much smaller and are not as finely detailed as those at other sites. The sheer number of panels, however, as well as the other attractions in the area, makes it an awesome destination. A trip down Nine Mile Canyon Road is like a trip through the history of the Southwest, as you pass rock art, stone dwellings, old homesteads, and telegraph poles originally installed by the famed "Buffalo Soldiers." Be sure to give yourself a full day to explore this incredible place.

5 BUCKHORN WASH ROCK-ART SITE

Bureau of Land Management
Price Field Office
125 South 600 West
Price, UT 84501
(435) 636-3600

NEAREST SUPPLY CENTER:
Green River, Utah

INTERPRETATION:
Interpretive panels

SEASONS OPEN: All seasons

HOURS OF OPERATION:
All hours

FEE AREA: No

ACCESS ROAD: Gravel

DIRECTIONS: Buckhorn Wash Rock-Art Panel is midway between the towns of Price and Green River. Traveling from Green River, drive 30 miles west on I-70 to Exit 129 and head north along a well-marked and maintained gravel road for approximately 27 miles to the site. The pictograph panel is 5.8 miles past the San Rafael campground.

Two ancient cultures, separated by thousands of years, created the 100-foot rock-art panel found at Buckhorn Wash. The first people to visit the area are believed to have been part of the Barrier Canyon culture. These nomads hunted, fished, and gathered plants throughout what is now known as southeastern Utah and along other regions on the Colorado Plateau. Experts believe these ancient people traveled for most of the year in small bands and, at certain times during the year, may have attended social and ceremonial gatherings held at Buckhorn Wash. During the Archaic period, more than 2,000 years ago, the people began to paint pictographs on the steep sandstone walls above the San Rafael River.

The black pigment is thought to have been made from a combination of sumac, yellow ochre, and piñon, vigorously mixed to create a powder. The yellow pigment seems to have been made from rabbitbrush, and the reds probably came from a mixture of red ochre and mountain mahogany roots. Plant oils or animal fats were used as bonding agents in the pigments. The people made paintbrushes from yucca fibers or hair and also blew paint onto the rock through reeds and hollow bird bones. The negative images at Buckhorn Wash, such as the many outlined handprints, are the result of this ancient blowing technique.

In addition to the colorful pictographs found at the wash, there is a sizable collection of petroglyphs thought to have been created by the more recent Southern San Rafael Fremont people who occupied the area between A.D. 600 and 1250. The Fremont artists used flint chisels and stone hammers to engrave their art into the red rock. Anthropomorphic figures and many zoomorphic images, including large mammals, reptiles, and birds, rest beside a series of geometric shapes of unknown meaning.

The natural setting in Buckhorn Wash is strikingly beautiful and worth a visit in and of itself. The rock-art site is remote, and your own exploration might uncover hidden sites or objects left by prehistoric people who roamed and camped in the area. Please leave these treasures where they lie.

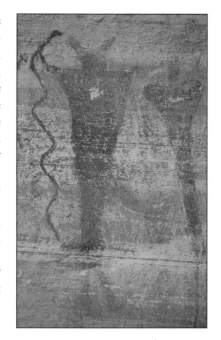

6 CAPITOL REEF NATIONAL PARK

HC 70 Box 15
Torrey, UT 84775-9602
(435) 425-3791

NEAREST SUPPLY CENTER:
Torrey, Utah

HIGHLIGHTS: The area around Capitol Reef National Park was once home to the Fremont people, who left traces of their culture behind on beautiful rock-art panels.

INTERPRETATION: Visitor center, educational programs, ranger-guided tours, and self-guided excursions

SEASONS OPEN: All seasons

HOURS OF OPERATION:
All hours (the visitor center is open from 8 a.m. to 4:30 p.m.)

FEE AREA: Yes

ACCESS ROAD: Paved

DIRECTIONS: Capitol Reef National Park is on UT 24 in south-central Utah, near the town of Torrey.

Middle Desert

It is hard to travel the remote backcountry of Capitol Reef National Park without feeling a sense of awe for the ancient people who once lived among the towering cliffs and immense sandstone formations here. Even today, the extensive wilderness in Capitol Reef represents some of the most remote and seldom-traveled land east of the Waterpocket Fold. The craggy and seemingly inhospitable landscape was formed hundreds of millions of years ago by sedimentary deposits in the ancient sea that once covered the area, and the sandstone surface was later sculpted by the flow of the Fremont River.

The ancient Fremont farmers settled in the Capitol Reef area as early as A.D. 700. They harvested crops and wild plants from the fertile floodplain and hunted mule deer, bighorn sheep, and rabbits. Despite the harsh environment, the Fremont people survived in the area for more than 600 years before abandoning their dwellings and fields.

Opposite: Cathedral Valley

Hickman Natural Bridge

The Fremont left few traces of their presence here, and much of what was left was later destroyed by early homesteaders, road building, and mining operations. However, the ancient rock art endures. The most accessible petroglyph panels are in the Fruita Historic District, a few miles from the park's visitor center. A wooden sidewalk winds its way along the base of the cliff and provides close views of the rock-art images, which include anthropomorphic figures as well as depictions of bighorn sheep and mule deer. The location of this petroglyph panel is of particular interest because it lies directly across from a beautiful field along the Fremont River. An ancient granary tucked under a sandstone overhang sits several miles up the road, suggesting that this field was once used by the Fremont farmers.

A trip through Capitol Reef National Park will expose you to a rich display of natural and human history, and the Bentonite Hills, Caineville Wash, and the Cathedral Valley areas offer a sense of remoteness found in few other national parks in the Southwest. The backcountry roads in the park can be traveled during most seasons but should be approached with caution if rain is in the forecast.

Cathedral Valley

7 ANASAZI STATE PARK

P.O. Box 1429
Boulder, UT 84716-1429
(435) 335-7308

NEAREST SUPPLY CENTER:
Boulder, Utah

HIGHLIGHTS: The Coombs Site, managed by the museum, was once home to a thriving Anasazi community.

INTERPRETATION: Museum, interpretive panels, and self-guided tours

SEASONS OPEN: All seasons

HOURS OF OPERATION:
8 a.m. to 6 p.m.

FEE AREA: Yes

ACCESS ROAD: Paved

DIRECTIONS: Anasazi State Park is in the town of Boulder in south-central Utah, which sits on UT 12 between the towns of Torrey and Escalante.

The ruins at Anasazi State Park represent a small section of what experts believe was, at one time, one of the largest Ancestral Puebloan (Anasazi) settlements on the southern slopes of the Aquarius Plateau. The Coombs Site, as it is now called, was built on a rough and broken landscape that supported human life for hundreds of years and still holds traces of the ancient culture.

Archaeologists believe that the Kayenta Anasazi migrated from southwestern Utah to the site here, settling in the high mountains around the plateau. The people irrigated and farmed the land, hunted wild game, and harvested native plants. Their culture thrived in this environment, and nearly 200 people may have lived in the village at its peak.

The partially excavated ruins at the Coombs Site include a 34-room, L-shaped pueblo that contained both residential and storage rooms. The living quarters face east and west and are significantly larger than the rooms used for storage, which face north and south. Both were accessed by hatchways in the roof or doors positioned high on the walls in an effort to keep rodents from entering the rooms.

There are two distinct types of prehistoric architecture found at the Coombs Site. The early people who lived here used jacal construction to build their pithouses. Thatched walls faced with small poles and thick mats of grass or sticks were plastered with layers of adobe

Pithouse Ruins

mud, and large wooden posts supported thatched roofs. The Kayenta-style masonry that replaced the pithouse structures is characterized by stone slabs and blocks held in place by thick layers of mud mortar and chinking stones.

The village is believed to have been occupied from A.D. 1050 to 1200, and seems to have been destroyed by fire. It is unclear whether the fire led to the village's abandonment, or whether the people set the fire when they left, but many experts believe the blaze reached a catastrophic level due to the highly flammable materials used in construction and the close proximity of the buildings here.

The first stage of scientific study at the Coombs Site was sponsored by Yale University's Peabody Museum in 1928 and was followed by a large-scale excavation by the University of Utah in 1958 as part of the Glen Canyon Salvage Project, which endeavored to catalog and interpret sites that might be impacted by the flooding of Glen Canyon. This study contributed greatly to our understanding of the ancient people who occupied the rugged plateaus and mountains of the Southwest. The site at Anasazi State Park covers an area of approximately 100 acres. To date, at least 100 structures have been identified by experts, but a substantial number of them remain buried—awaiting future excavation and new discovery.

Pueblo Ruins

8 SEGO CANYON ROCK-ART SITE

Bureau of Land Management
Moab Field Office
82 E. Dogwood Ave.
Moab, UT 84532
(435) 259-2100

NEAREST SUPPLY CENTER:
Thompson Springs, Utah

HIGHLIGHTS: The rock art at Sego Canyon represents the work of artists from three different cultures and archaeological periods.

INTERPRETATION:
Interpretive panels

SEASONS OPEN: All seasons

HOURS OF OPERATION:
All hours

FEE AREA: No

ACCESS ROAD: Paved

DIRECTIONS: Sego Canyon Rock-Art Site is 4 miles north of the town of Thompson Springs in east-central Utah, just off I-70. Proceed north through the small town and across the railroad tracks, and look for a sign for Sego Canyon Petroglyphs just past the northern edge of town.

The rock art at Sego Canyon provides an interesting point for comparing the rock-art styles of the Southwest. The three separate panels here represent the work of three distinct cultures, yet the similarities between the images display the timeless influence these native people had on those who came before and after them.

The first panel (east-facing) is believed to have been painted by the artists of the Barrier Canyon culture, which is responsible for some of the most spectacular rock art in the Southwest. Experts believe these nomads may have used the Sego Canyon site as a temporary camp during their seasonal travels more than 6,000 years ago. The ancient hunters did not inhabit permanent structures here, but they are believed to have stayed in caves and crudely constructed brush shelters along the migration paths of wild game. The Barrier Canyon art depicts anthropomorphic beings with an almost ghostlike quality; the hollow eye sockets and absence of human arms and legs gives these figures an otherworldly appearance. The panel was painted with natural pigments and features 19 figures, some of which appear to have horns, branching antennae, or decorative headdresses.

The paintings on the south-facing cliffs at Sego Canyon exhibit Fremont art as it evolved over the centuries. This panel includes two distinct examples of Fremont petroglyphs superimposed over earlier anthropomorphic figures painted in red pigment. The second series of petroglyphs on this panel include bighorn sheep and other more recent designs pecked alongside and over the older Fremont work. The Fremont panel at Sego Canyon is an excellent example of the successive reuse of an area over time and the chronological development of Fremont rock art in general.

Across the wash, directly in front of the parking lot, is an outstanding sample of more contemporary rock art, painted by the Ute. This group of petroglyphs includes human figures mounted on horses, which can be dated by the introduction of the horse to the Ute people by the Spanish in the late 16th century. Other human figures are seen dressed in leggings or carrying round shields. The image of a large white bison at Sego Canyon has significant spiritual meaning for the Ute.

Early Ute people (Notah) were hunter-gatherers, which is probably why hunting plays such a central role in their art. Like the Barrier Canyon people before them, they were drawn to the area around Sego Canyon because of the abundant wildlife and plant life here. The Ute hunted with the bow and arrow and lived in small, temporary brush dwellings known as *wickiups,* continuing to live a nomadic existence in southeastern Utah and western Colorado until they were confined to reservations in 1880.

9 ARCHES NATIONAL PARK

P.O. Box 907
Moab, UT 84532-0907
(435) 719-2299

NEAREST SUPPLY CENTER:
Moab, Utah

HIGHLIGHTS: The red-rock walls at Arches are steeped in natural and human history. Pictographs and petroglyphs spanning several cultures adorn the sandstone, telling a saga of human presence here.

INTERPRETATION: Visitor center, interpretive panels, and self-guided tours

SEASONS OPEN: All seasons

HOURS OF OPERATION:
All hours (The visitor center is open from 8 a.m. to 4:30 p.m., with longer hours from spring through fall.)

FEE AREA: Yes

ACCESS ROAD: Paved

DIRECTIONS: Arches National Park is north of the town of Moab, on US 191.

Landscape Arch

The backcountry of Arches National Park is a natural maze of stalwart sandstone formations rising up from the desert floor. Despite the striking beauty here, the setting appears uninhabitable by today's standards. However, this territory was home to indigenous people for thousands of years, beginning with the nomadic hunters, gatherers, and farmers of Archaic times.

What a strange and spiritual place Arches must have been for those early visitors as they traveled across the open countryside! Archaeologists believe the barren region was once the hunting and gathering ground for the Ancestral Puebloan (Anasazi) people, who inhabited lands to the south of the park, and the ancient Fremont people, indigenous to regions north of Arches. Much later, Ute people migrated through the area and came into contact with Spanish explorers. A visual history of these diverse cultures was left behind on rock-art panels in Arches.

Petroglyph panels can be found along many of the remote backcountry trails that wind their way among the towering spires of Arches. These petroglyphs, which are generally found on the flat surfaces of sandstone cliffs, rock overhangs, or freestanding boulders, depict zoomorphic figures like mule deer,

Opposite: Turret Arch

bighorn sheep, and a variety of smaller animals as well as elaborate hunting scenes with humanlike figures poised in the chase. A variety of geometric symbols and shapes appear as well and carry unknown meanings.

The petroglyphs in Arches were created by Anasazi artists who chiseled the images into the sandstone by either striking it with a sharp, hard rock or by tapping a chisel-like tool with a heavy stone. Though slower, the second method created a much clearer image and perhaps was only employed when time allowed between long hunting excursions. One of the most accessible petroglyph panels at Arches lies in the Wolfe Ranch area along the trail to the famous Delicate Arch. This site features a large herd of bighorn sheep being chased by human hunters.

The Fremont people were more inclined to make use of natural paints to create their art, called pictographs. The red paint they used most frequently consisted of crushed hematite mixed with a bonding agent made from human or animal blood and sometimes animal or vegetable oils. The paint was applied to the sandstone surface with brushes made of yucca fibers or hair. Pigment was also blown onto the sandstone through narrow reeds or tiny bird bones. Many of the pictographs at the park depict large, trapezoidal, or round-bodied

Delicate Arch

humanoids, oftentimes appearing ghostlike as they hover on the cliff faces. Many of these images are believed to be more than 900 years old.

The Ute people also left their mark on the rocks here as they passed through the area on hunting excursions. Their images of men on horseback can be seen mingling with the Anasazi art at the petroglyph panel near Wolfe Ranch.

Even after considerable study, experts hesitate to interpret the meaning of the ancient rock-art images at Arches or to speculate about why the Anasazi, Fremont, and Ute people chose to leave their artwork in these places. While no dwellings have been discovered in the park, some of the panels are close to natural springs, seeps, or areas used as hunting camps or ceremonial sites. Perhaps these places were spiritually significant to the people whose art adorns the walls.

Rock art at Wolfe Ranch

Balanced Rock

10 MOAB ROCK-ART SITES

Moab Area Travel Council
P.O. Box 550
Moab, UT 84532
(800) 635-6622

NEAREST SUPPLY CENTER:
Moab, Utah

HIGHLIGHTS: These rock-art sites are easily accessed by car and lie just a stone's throw from the town of Moab.

INTERPRETATION: Interpretive panels exist at some of the sites. Stop for information at the Grand County Travel/Moab Visitor Center at Center and Main Streets.

SEASONS OPEN: All seasons

HOURS OF OPERATION: All hours

FEE AREA: No

ACCESS ROAD: Paved

DIRECTIONS: Moab is located on US 191 in east-central Utah. Directions to individual sites are included in the site descriptions.

Moab, Utah, is a quaint town located just a few miles south of Arches National Park. Moab's rock-art sites represent an interesting mix of artistic styles associated with Ancestral Puebloan (Anasazi), Fremont, and more contemporary Ute people—all of whom either roamed through or lived in the area since prehistoric times. Three easily accessible sites are close to town. Just ask for directions at the information center in the heart of town.

The Fremont people arrived in the area around what we now know today as Arches and Canyonlands National Parks and the Colorado River area sometime between A.D. 600 and 1250. The southern boundary of the Fremont homeland borders the northern fringe of the sweeping Ancestral Puebloan country, which accounts for the cultural mix found in the rock art here. This blending of cultures is not only apparent in the style of rock art but also extends to pottery, household items, hunting implements, tools, weapons, and other artifacts uncovered in the area.

As the Fremont culture waned in the late 1200s, the Anasazi people began to thrive and swiftly spread across much of the vast region. Later, the Ute spent

Potash Road petroglyphs

Opposite: Merrimac Butte

time in the area as they followed the herds across the Southwest. During the time of their presence in the regions, these cultures left their marks on the red sandstone cliffs, portraying their diversity through pictures ranging from hand-prints and geometric shapes to human figures, animals, and hunting scenes.

The **Potash Panels** are on Utah 279 (Potash Road) just outside of town. Travel north on US 191 (toward Arches National Park) and look for a sign for Potash Road/UT 279 on the left side of the highway after roughly four miles. Turn left at the junction, and travel nine miles along the Colorado River. Look for signs for "Indian Writings" beneath the steep sandstone cliffs.

A number of anthropomorphic figures, some carrying shields and what appear to be lances or spears, are featured at this site. Several of the human figures are adorned with ceremonial headdresses and round ear bobs. There are also a number of animal images, including a spectacular rendering of a bear, pecked into the dark sandstone veneer at the first pullout. Deer, elk, and bighorn sheep are also depicted at the site. Abstract forms are plentiful and include numerous geometric symbols. The Potash Panels display a mixture of both Fremont art and images associated with the Anasazi culture. A mounted horseman, probably crafted by a Ute artist, is also featured here.

The site at **Courthouse Wash** is four miles north of Moab on US 191. Along the way, you'll cross bridges over the Colorado River and Courthouse Wash; look for a parking lot on the right, a few hundred feet past the Courthouse Wash bridge. A well-marked trail leads back across the bridge and proceeds for another half-mile to the site, which is on the cliff face above the highway. Look for the rock-art panels and information signs at the base of the steep cliffs.

Courthouse Wash petroglyphs

The site includes a large panel of paintings associated with the Barrier Canyon culture, which experts believe predates the arrival of the Fremont people by thousands of years. The pictographs include two anthropomorphic images that appear to be holding large, round, white objects—possibly shields. The images were painted on the stone surfaces with natural pigments. Red ochre and mountain mahogany roots were mixed to make the red tint visible on the panel. The figures appear to be wearing hats or pointed horns, both characteristic of these ancient paintings. Fremont artists pecked their art into the rock faces at the foot of the panel, adding their petroglyphs to the pictograph display. The Courthouse Wash site was severely vandalized, but significant and costly refurbishing has been done so that visitors are able to enjoy the fragile images today.

The **Golf Course** site is so named because of its proximity to the greens. The small site is roughly four miles south of Moab on US 191. When you see the golf course on the right, turn left on Spanish Trail Road and proceed for a mile to Westwater Drive. Turn right and continue for about a half-mile to a pullout and a three-rail fence enclosing the small cliff face. The Golf Course site is made up exclusively of petroglyphs, most of which were done by Fremont artists, with some scattered images left by the Anasazi. The ornate headdresses, horns, and ear bobs on some of the human images are typical of the Fremont era, and bighorn sheep, deer, and elk are contrasted by several abstract designs.

The petroglyphs reach close to 30 feet up the eroded sandstone wall. Even though the panel has deteriorated somewhat over time, the images have survived the harsh effects of the desert environment well, echoing the endurance of the people who painted them.

Golf Course petroglyphs

11 CANYONLANDS NATIONAL PARK

2282 SW Resource Blvd.
Moab, UT 84532
(435) 719-2313

NEAREST SUPPLY CENTER:
Moab, Utah

HIGHLIGHTS: Canyonlands National Park is a geological masterpiece. Yet traces of a human past lie hidden within the red cliffs, spires, and canyons as well, awaiting your discovery.

INTERPRETATION:
Visitor centers, exhibits, and self-guided tours

SEASONS OPEN: All seasons

HOURS OF OPERATION:
All hours (visitor centers are open from 8 a.m. to 4:30 p.m. daily)

FEE AREA: Yes

ACCESS ROAD: Paved to some areas; gravel road to Horseshoe Canyon

DIRECTIONS: Canyonlands National Park is in southeastern Utah and can be accessed from a number of different locations. UT 211, north of Monticello, leads to the visitor center in the Needles District, and UT 313, north of Moab, leads to the visitor center and sites within the Island in the Sky District. Backcountry sites are accessed via unpaved roads, and specific directions can be secured at one of the visitor centers.

Roadside Ruins, Needles District

The spectacular beauty of Canyonlands National Park is marked by deep, twisting canyons, the flowing waters of the Green and Colorado Rivers, and broad mesas stretching as far as the eye can see. The rugged, fractured landscape here is the work of millions of years of wind and water erosion and appears inhospitable to human existence. However, a closer look at the steep canyon recesses reveals the remains of an enduring period of indigenous occupation extending back to 7000 B.C., when Archaic hunters and gatherers roamed the canyon country.

Canyonlands National Park is divided into three districts: the Island in the Sky, the Needles, and the Maze. The Horseshoe Canyon area, a separate unit to the northwest, is also part of the park. Rock-art panels are scattered throughout the backcountry in these areas, and a number of archaeological sites are accessible as well.

Cave Spring, Needles District

A drive through the **Needles District** leads to two prehistoric ruin sites, Roadside Ruin and Tower Ruin, and an accessible display of rock art at Cave Springs. These sites are not far from the Needles Visitor Center and are good places to start your exploration.

Horseshoe Canyon, also known as Barrier Canyon, hosts one of the largest and most dramatic rock-art displays in the Southwest. The pictographs in the Great Gallery represent one of the most concentrated collections of the Fremont people's Barrier Canyon–style rock art to be found anywhere in the region. The site at Horseshoe Canyon also includes some of the oldest pictographic art found in the Southwest, dating back

Cave Spring pictographs

to Archaic times. Fortunately, this collection of panels is protected to some degree by its remoteness, and a considerable amount of hiking and exploration is necessary to reach the images.

A hiker can find rich displays of pictographs, petroglyphs, and ruin sites just about anywhere within the canyon recesses. As you visit the more remote locations in the park, however, be very careful not to tread on the cryptobiotic soil. This dark, crusty earth serves as the foundation for high-desert plant life and is extremely important to the health of the ecosystem here. It is also important to be mindful of rattlesnakes in this area. Stop at one of the park's visitor centers to learn about treading lightly through the backcountry at Canyonlands.

Shafer Canyon Overlook

It was midmorning before we left our Peekaboo campsite to hike our way into Squaw Canyon. Over the years, Cathie and I have grown accustomed to surveying the steep sandstone walls of Canyonlands National Park for signs of ancient rock art; we have learned by experience that there are still unmarked sites here, and finding them requires patience and sharp eyes.

The deep canyons and open washes of the interior of Canyonlands seem to vibrate with messages from the past. As we explore the backcountry here, it is impossible not to sense the presence of its ancient inhabitants and to feel a sense of awe at their ability to survive within this dense canyon country hundreds of years ago.

The sun bakes down on my hat-covered head as I cross open washes and thread my way beside sandstone cliffs as high as modern skyscrapers, and I wonder about the ancient people's need for shade, food, and water. What would it have been like to call this harsh and wondrous place home?

The pictographs here inspire me, too. I often ponder their meanings and wonder if the images offer explanations—answers to my own questions and to those of archaeologists who've spent a lifetime studying the ruins and rock art here. How are we to read these ancient messages? Who were they intended for?

Each night, after we spent the day hiking and taking photographs of this amazing landscape, Cathie and I returned to the comfort of our modern world and took time to share our discoveries. After our day in Canyonlands, we had a lot to talk about. Our reverence for the people who once lived here, and the almost palpable presence we both felt as we wandered through the red-rock spires and shadowed canyons, has left an indelible imprint on our memories.

Peekaboo Canyon

12 NEWSPAPER ROCK

P.O. Box 788
Blanding, UT 84511-0788
(435) 678-2238

NEAREST SUPPLY CENTER:
Monticello, Utah

HIGHLIGHTS: Newspaper
Rock reports the presence
of a mixture of indigenous
cultures that passed through
or settled this region of the
Southwest. It is one of the
most easily accessible rock-
art sites in the area.

INTERPRETATION: None

SEASONS OPEN: All seasons

HOURS OF OPERATION:
All hours

FEE AREA: No

ACCESS ROAD TYPE: Paved

DIRECTIONS: Newspaper Rock
is 51 miles south of Moab and
14 miles north of Monticello
on UT 211. From the intersection of US 191 and UT 211,
head west for 9 miles on
UT 211 toward the Needles
District of Canyonlands
National Park. The parking
lot for the Newspaper Rock
site is clearly marked. Shay
Creek, a smaller site, is 2 miles
farther west and unmarked.
Look for a small pullout on
the side of the road.

Experts believe the Archaic people, nomads who wandered through the Four Corners area more than 8,000 years ago, were the first to etch markings in the dark desert varnish covering Newspaper Rock. These travelers hunted animals and collected plants along the streambed and in the high mountains surrounding the site. The people first inhabited caves and crudely constructed brush huts that they built along their route, but all that remains of their presence here are faint signs of their art at Newspaper Rock.

The San Rafael Fremont people occupied the area after the Archaic hunters and pecked humanlike figures with large trapezoidal bodies and small heads onto the rock walls here. Their depictions of bighorn sheep, deer, elk, and other animals appear to roam at will across the busy rock-art panel. Scholars who have studied Newspaper Rock believe these animal figures were created sometime between A.D. 600 and 1250. Ancestral Puebloan (Anasazi) artists left their mark on the large panel as well, probably sometime after the Fremont people had left the area. Specific images, such as the mounted riders attributed to Ute or Navajo artists, help to date the work found on these panels. These figures must have been created after Spanish conquistadors introduced the horse to the Southwest during the 16th century.

Experts have identified between 200 and 300 separate images on the complex panel at Newspaper Rock. As you look at the petroglyphs, notice how the work seems to improve as time went on, transforming from the stick people designed by early artists into fully formed human figures in action. The animal forms seemed to have evolved in style as well, and many are pictured in groups, possibly in an effort to tell a story. Footprints are also common on the panel, as are an abundance of abstract images of unknown meaning.

Some people believe that the pictographs and petroglyphs of the Southwest were more than art, but that they were actually used as a way of message sending—an ancient newspaper of sorts. If this theory is true (as Newspaper Rock's name would suggest) the site here is certainly the Sunday edition!

When I first stood in front of Newspaper Rock, the thing that impressed me most was just how much time is represented by the art on the boulder's surface. Thousands of years have come and gone since the first people etched messages on the rock here, spanning the presence of archaic nomads to that of Spanish settlers.

As I look at the physical environment around the rock, I try to imagine what made this place special—why the people chose to leave a record of their presence here in this very spot. Perhaps the area held spiritual meaning for them, or it was a convenient place to stop on a trade or travel route. We'll never truly know, but it is fun to speculate about the meaning behind the images here. A picture—or in this case a pictograph or petroglyph—is truly worth a thousand words.

13 EDGE OF THE CEDARS STATE PARK

660 West 400 North
Blanding, UT 84511-4000
(435) 678-2238

NEAREST SUPPLY CENTER:
Blanding, Utah

HIGHLIGHTS: The museum at
Edge of the Cedars contains
one of the largest collections
of ceramic vessels on display
in the Southwest, and the
archaeological site tells the
story of Ancestral Puebloan
occupation here.

INTERPRETATION: Museum
and self-guided tour

SEASONS OPEN: All seasons

HOURS OF OPERATION:
Summer, 8 a.m. to 7 p.m.;
winter, 9 a.m. to 5 p.m.

FEE AREA: Yes

ACCESS ROAD: Paved

DIRECTIONS: Edge of the
Cedars State Park is in the
southeast corner of Utah in
the town of Blanding, along
US 191. Once in Blanding,
the route to the Edge of the
Cedars museum is clearly
marked.

The structures that remain at Edge of the Cedars are believed to have been built and occupied from A.D. 825 to 1220. Like many other archaeological sites in the Cedar Mesa region, the village at the Edge of the Cedars exemplifies the continuous social and cultural growth of the Ancestral Puebloans (Anasazi) during the 400 years that they inhabited the area.

The early Anasazi first lived in subterranean pithouses they excavated in the rocky ground and relied on their hunting and gathering skills for food. These prehistoric people also began to farm the land here, using techniques they learned from cultures south of Cedar Mesa. As their agriculture progressed and their society evolved, the Anasazi began replacing their pithouses with above-ground pueblo structures.

The pueblo village is situated on a small ridge above the Westwater Creek drainage, which provided the ancient farmers with a good source of water for their crops. They built small irrigation systems that diverted water into shallow ditches and onto the mineral-rich soil where their corn, squash, and beans thrived.

It is believed that the ancient people who inhabited this site harvested and stored crops only once during a growing season, so a year's food supply infested by insects, rodents, or rainwater would have been devastating to the people. As a result, the safe storage of crops and other food was one of the most important functions of the pueblo. Surface granaries, constructed with blocks of sandstone and thick layers of clay mortar, kept foodstuffs safe from floods and infestations that would have destroyed goods stored in pithouses.

Despite this architectural shift, a single village unit remained below the ground. The Anasazi believed they came to this earth from a world beneath, and the ceremonial kiva provided a spiritual connection to their subterranean past. The *sipapu*, a small hole dug in the floor of the kiva, is thought to have symbolized the place from which their ancestors emerged.

The pueblo ruins seen today at Edge of the Cedars are just a small corner of a large village, most of which has not been excavated. As many as 250 people are thought to have occupied the site, which may have included 10 separate kivas as well as a Great Kiva. A trail leaves from the museum and threads its way through the site, with interpretive panels to guide you along the way.

14 CAVE TOWER RUINS

Bureau of Land Management
Monticello Field Office
435 N. Main St./P.O. Box 7
Monticello, UT 84535
(435) 587-1500

NEAREST SUPPLY CENTER:
Blanding, Utah

HIGHLIGHTS: Cave Tower is
one of several towers in the
Cedar Mesa area that may
have been constructed as a
means for communication
between the ancient pueblo
villages.

INTERPRETATION: None

SEASONS OPEN: All seasons

HOURS OF OPERATION:
All hours

FEE AREA: No

ACCESS ROAD: Rough gravel,
impassable after heavy rain
or snow. A high-clearance
vehicle is recommended.

DIRECTIONS: Cave Tower Ruins
is on UT 95, 20 miles west of
its intersection with US 191
and 16 miles east of Natural
Bridges National Monument.
The small dirt road leading
to Cave Tower Ruins is at
mile marker 103, just 0.7 mile
east of the turnoff for Mule
Canyon Ruins. Travel south
along the dirt road for about
2 miles until it appears to run
out at a small pullout. The
tower is on the ridge overlooking the wash to the left.

Well-preserved Cave Tower is worth the adventure required to find it. From its picturesque vantage point above the deep, cliff-lined wash, the tower is a very impressive site. Cave Tower catches the first rays of morning light and glows like a beacon among the large boulders that form its foundation. The presence of other towers in the area, all built along the same line of sight, leads archaeologists to believe that Cave Tower was part of a signaling system used by the ancient people to communicate between pueblo villages. (While you're at Cave Tower, look for the tower at Mule Canyon Ruins, roughly one mile to the west.)

Experts believe Cave Tower was probably constructed between A.D. 750 and 900. It was during this time that surface dwellings and storage structures, rather than subterranean pithouses, became the most common architectural style of the Ancestral Puebloan (Anasazi) people.

The base rock layers surrounding the ruins and much of the flat land around them are marked with thousands of dish-shaped potholes. Rain and snowmelt was collected in these depressions and then scooped into crude ceramic vessels that were stored in shaded rooms within the pueblos. Water was also transported to the village sites from the sandy wash below, which some experts believe flowed more consistently during ancient times than it does today.

The environment around the tower was abundant with natural plants and herbs that the people used for both food and medicinal purposes. The ancient farmers also grew crops on the flat mesas along the wash and hunted in the thick forests and brushy washes for mule deer and rabbits.

During their occupation here, the pottery skills of the ancient people increased dramatically, and

Mule deer

pots became more decorative and intricate. This fact, along with the ongoing development of other crafts, including woven textiles, indicates to experts that the Anasazi at Cave Tower enjoyed a more sedentary lifestyle as their agriculture developed.

Today, it is hard to imagine why a group of people took years to build solid stone structures like Cave Tower and the many other pueblo villages that surround it, only to pack up their belongings one day and migrate southward. But tree-ring dating performed on many of the Cedar Mesa and Grand Gulch sites reveals that, around A.D. 1250, the Puebloan people stopped building and left their villages behind shortly thereafter.

Some feel the migration was brought on by the arrival of fierce enemies, while others hold to the theory that dramatic changes in climate and shifts in seasonal rainfall drove the people from the mesas. Perhaps we'll never know why the Anasazi abandoned the stone villages around Cedar Mesa and Grand Gulch, leaving these lonely towers as testaments to their time here.

We wanted to catch the ruins at Cave Tower at sunrise in order to photograph the brightly colored rocks and walls against the deep blue sky. The road in was hard to follow, as it crossed a number of solid sandstone benches and seemed to disappear for stretches on the rock surface, especially in the early light of dawn.

We reached the end of the road about a half-hour before the sun came up, and we began to search for the ruins in the half-light. Fortunately, Cave Tower wasn't hard to find. We'd been told that it sat on the brink of a wash overlooking a large area, and that it had been used to communicate with the tower at Mule Canyon Ruins. We took a compass reading at the Mule Canyon Tower and came close to pinpointing our destination. As morning broke, we were treated to the bright, golden rays of the eastern sun as it rose over the flat country surrounding the ruin site. Dawn lit up the crumbling stone structure, making it gleam like a mystic castle.

Cave Tower stands alone on the edge of a rock-lined wash, as if to survey the landscape. As we watched it materialize in the rising sun, it was easy for us to imagine the tower serving as a lookout for the hundreds of sites tucked in the gulches, washes, and shadowed alcoves below. After we'd taken full advantage of the spectacular light on the tower and shot a number of images, Cathie sat beside the ruins, enjoying the scenery and solitude. I explored the area for other sites farther up the wash and tried to imagine what life would have been like when this area hosted a bustling community centuries ago. We were both inspired by our time here and intrigued by the mysterious tower built so long ago.

15 BUTLER WASH RUINS

Bureau of Land Management
Monticello Field Office
435 N. Main St./P.O. Box 7
Monticello, UT 84535
(435) 587-1500

NEAREST SUPPLY CENTER:
Blanding, Utah

HIGHLIGHTS: The cliff dwelling
at Butler Wash sits in a large
sandstone alcove and is one
of the most beautifully sited
ruins in southeastern Utah.

INTERPRETATION: None

SEASONS OPEN: All seasons

HOURS OF OPERATION:
All hours

FEE AREA: No

ACCESS ROAD TYPE: Paved

DIRECTIONS: The Butler Wash
Ruins site is just off UT 95,
approximately 10.5 miles
west of its intersection with
US 191. The turnoff for Butler
Wash is well marked. A one-
mile trail departs from the
parking lot and follows the
rim of Butler Wash, leading
to a fenced overlook.

The prehistoric cliff dwelling, perched above the lushly carpeted Butler Wash, is all that remains of the Ancestral Puebloan (Anasazi) people who once thrived here. The structures at Butler Wash are believed to have been built and occupied sometime between A.D. 1100 and 1300 and are similar to those found at Mesa Verde and Canyon de Chelly.

Villages in the Cedar Mesa area followed two distinct architectural styles during this time. Freestanding pueblos, large enough to house a significant number of residents, were constructed in the canyon bottoms and on the rims, while cliff dwellings were built in the cavelike alcoves high on sandstone cliffs. These villages were accessed by long wooden ladders or handholds and footholds carved into the steep sandstone walls.

Defense seemed to be of great importance to the people of Butler Wash. They may have had to compete with other villages in the Cedar Mesa area for food, due to dramatic climatic changes, overhunting, or the depletion of natural resources, and the resulting strife could have produced a need for cliff dwellings, which were easy to defend. Another possible reason for the rise in defensible villages might have been the southern migration of warlike nomadic tribes.

The cliff dwellings included many living chambers and storage rooms as well as four ceremonial kivas, suggesting that a large number of people resided here. The village faces south and takes advantage of the warmth provided by the low angle of the winter sun. This solar heat must have been important to the residents here, due to the harsh winters common in the Cedar Mesa area. Fresh water, which ran over the lip of the alcove and trickled down into the dwelling, was also a unique amenity at the Butler Wash dwelling. Excess water from rainstorms and seasonal snowmelt was collected and used to irrigate crops cultivated along the wash.

Artifacts uncovered at Butler Wash, such as potsherds and other household items, reveal the significant cultural advances the Anasazi made during their time here. It was during this period that they began creating the thin-walled, highly polished vessels that came to be known as Mesa Verde Black-on-White pottery. Woven cotton textiles also became more prevalent during this time. Some experts believe these artistic advancements indicate that the people had leisure time in which to pursue their crafts—a direct result of their agricultural success.

Despite the cultural advances, however, existence was hard for the Anasazi, to say the least. Life in the cliff dwellings subjected the ancient people to frequent epidemics, including parasite infestation from household dogs and turkeys. Poor ventilation in the cliff dwellings, especially during the winter, is thought to have caused respiratory problems such as pneumonia and influenza as well. High childhood death rates were also common, with a staggering 50 percent mortality rate among children, and most of these early deaths came before the age of six. It was probably drought, however, that eventually forced the Anasazi to abandon their beautiful cliff dwellings and prosperous fields at Butler Wash and migrate to new farmlands in New Mexico and Arizona.

The first time we visited the ruins at Butler Wash it was in the last hour of evening light, and the low angle of the sun set everything around the ruins aglow. Unfortunately for us, the ruins are tucked away within the darkened alcove and refused to creep from behind the dense shadows that had already

consumed the lower reaches of the wash. It is tricky in places like Butler Wash to get the light just right and manage to create visually impressive images to boot.

The next morning at nine o'clock, the first rays of sunlight touched the upper lip of the alcove where the cliff dwellings sit. As the sunlight crept slowly down the face of the cliff and across the alcove, it looked like a slowly opening curtain set before a theater stage. An hour later, the whole wash basked in the bright, warm rays, giving us an hour of good imagemaking before the whole thing happened in reverse as the sun traveled to the opposite side of the wash.

Even the sparkling grains of sand within the red-rock walls seemed to dance before our camera lenses, as if to show us how time and nature had transformed them over the eons—smoothing, carving, and compressing—as it sculpted the rugged landscape.

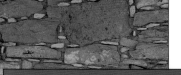

16 MULE CANYON RUINS

Bureau of Land Management
Monticello Field Office
435 N. Main St./P.O. Box 7
Monticello, Utah 84535
(435) 587-1500

NEAREST SUPPLY CENTER:
Blanding, Utah

HIGHLIGHTS: The site at
Mule Canyon Ruins is well
maintained and features a
number of excavated pueblo
structures. Interpretive panels
provide information about
the area and the Anasazi
people who once lived here.

INTERPRETATION:
Interpretive panels

SEASONS OPEN: All seasons

HOURS OF OPERATION:
All hours

FEE AREA: No

ACCESS ROAD: Paved

DIRECTIONS: The Mule Canyon
Ruins site is on UT 95, 20
miles west of its intersection
with US 191 and 16 miles east
of Natural Bridges National
Monument. The pullout, on
the north side of the highway,
is clearly marked.

The pueblo village at Mule Canyon is thought to have been first occupied around A.D. 750, but it was soon abandoned. The primary and longest-lasting occupation of the village came much later, when the Ancestral Puebloan (Anasazi) people moved back into the site between A.D. 1000 and 1500.

Artifacts recovered in Mule Canyon indicate that the ancient people who resided here were influenced by the prehistoric people living to the southeast, around the area now known as Mesa Verde. Various traits associated with the Kayenta Anasazi of what is now northwestern Arizona are also apparent in pottery fragments recovered during the excavation. These outside influences point to the dramatic impact the trade networks had on the cultural evolution of the Southwest.

The main ruin here is a 12-room pueblo, once consisting of both above- and below-ground structures. The excavated pueblo is believed to have been home to two or three family groups during prehistoric times and used primarily for sleeping and storage. The inhabitants probably entered the rooms through roof hatchways and used ladders to get in and out of their living quarters. When weather conditions on Cedar Mesa permitted, and especially during the summer months, cooking and other daily activities took place on the flat rooftops of the dwellings or in the central plaza in front of the living quarters.

The remnants of two additional stone structures lie southeast of the apartment-style rooms. A large, round, underground kiva, complete with a fire pit and

ventilation shaft, is thought to have hosted spiritual ceremonies and community gatherings at the village. Toward the center of the kiva, the ancient people dug a small hole called a *sipapu*, representing the place through which the spiritual ancestors of the Anasazi first emerged. The thatched roof enclosing the kiva was supported by large juniper logs. These timbers were crossed with smaller poles, sticks, and brush and coated with thick layers of adobe mud, which hardened in the hot summer sun. A small hatchway was left in the roof for entry.

The round foundation on the far edge of the kiva is believed to have supported a circular, two-story adobe tower built with large stone blocks and slabs. An underground tunnel links this structure to the kiva's interior. The purpose of the tower is still unknown; however, some scholars believe it shared the ceremonial function of the kiva or was used for solar observation. Others believe the stone tower was used to communicate between the villages in the area. This theory is supported by the fact that the Mule Canyon Tower was built in direct line of sight with the Cave Tower, situated on the mesa one mile to the southeast. Perhaps people in these towers passed messages of warning between villages.

Adventurous explorers can look for a smaller ruin site hidden in the alcove walls above Mule Canyon Wash, just north of the main ruin. Two single-story structures tucked in the side of the cliff may have housed farming families or served as field houses during the growing season.

Tree-ring analysis indicates that the Anasazi began to leave the area around southeastern Utah around A.D. 1250. But why did the ancient people abandon their sturdy homes and the seemingly abundant resources of Mule Canyon? This question continues to fuel archaeological studies today. Their departure may have been spawned by climatic changes within the region, such as prolonged drought or dramatic shifts in the seasonal pattern of rainfall. Although their diet was supplemented by wild game, native plants, and domestically raised turkeys, the people of Mule Canyon were dependent on cultivated crops like corn, beans, and squash, and prolonged drought would have greatly impacted agriculture here. Erosion, soil depletion, overhunting, and destruction of forest resources could have also complicated life in the Cedar Mesa area, causing the people to search for more fertile land.

Some experts believe fierce nomadic tribes arrived in the area, making defense a primary concern for the early inhabitants. More than likely, the abandonment of Cedar Mesa and pueblo villages like the one at Mule Canyon resulted from a combination of these hardships. Perhaps future archaeological discoveries will bring us closer to the answer.

It felt like we had stumbled across an ancient dwelling that had yet to be discovered in this little alcove, just north of the large ruin site at Mule Canyon. Though it was hidden behind the tall cottonwoods at the base of the wash, Cathie and I were able to see the faint outline of a stone wall in a shaded alcove above the trail. Thrilled with our seeming discovery, we climbed the rocky slope without stopping to rest and arrived at the alcove out of breath from exertion and excitement.

Small stones littered the floor of the alcove, and a thick layer of dusty sand covered everything; it was as if nothing had been disturbed here for a long time. We approached the stone walls slowly, half expecting the ghosts of the people who once lived here to come fluttering out as we drew near, and peeked through the square windows into lightless rooms.

Both Cathie and I experienced a strange and inexplicable sensation as we explored the ruins here, our cameras gripped tightly in anticipation and wonder. We felt as if we were recording a new discovery—cataloging the relics of a lost generation of people who had mysteriously disappeared. We treaded lightly through the ruins, watching, experiencing, and witnessing the indescribable magic of this place.

Another mystery of the northern alcove at Mule Canyon exposed itself a month later, after the images returned from our processing lab. In each of the images we took, light glowed across the roof of the alcove and cascaded down over the ruins. Neither Cathie nor I remember seeing this strange phenomenon while we were exploring and photographing the ruins, and we have no explanation for its presence in our images. Like so many things about the ruins of the Southwest, this ethereal light remains a mystery.

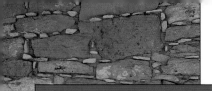

17 NATURAL BRIDGES NATIONAL MONUMENT

HC 60 Box 1
Lake Powell, UT 84533-0101
(435) 692-1234

NEAREST SUPPLY CENTER:
Blanding, Utah

HIGHLIGHTS: The remote ruins at Natural Bridges National Monument represent a well-preserved chapter in the story of the Anasazi people, and the monument itself is a geological wonderland!

INTERPRETATION:
Visitor center, interpretive panels, and self-guided auto and hiking tours

SEASONS OPEN: All seasons

HOURS OF OPERATION:
The scenic drive is open from sunrise to sunset daily

FEE AREA: Yes

ACCESS ROAD: Paved

DIRECTIONS: Natural Bridges National Monument is 42 miles southwest of Blanding. The entrance to the monument is at the end of UT 275, which is just off UT 95.

Horsecollar Ruins

Natural Bridges National Monument is tucked within Utah's spectacular White Canyon. The area is renowned for three natural bridges that span the full width of the White Canyon Wash. In order to protect these impressive formations, Theodore Roosevelt designated the area a National Monument in 1908. The boundaries of the monument were expanded shortly thereafter in order to include several important archaeological sites associated with the Ancestral Puebloan (Anasazi) culture. The names of the bridges were changed to the Hopi words Kachina, Sipapu, and Owachomo in order to honor the important history of native people in the area.

Aside from the spectacular beauty of its formations and deeply cut canyons, Natural Bridges National Monument hosts a formidable record of prehistoric life. The saga begins with the Archaic people who may have traveled among the canyon walls as early as 7000 B.C., leaving little behind to mark their presence here besides a few stone tools. These people were thought to have been followed by the Basketmakers around A.D. 100, and later by the Anasazi, who moved into the area and built homes on the mesatops above the canyon in roughly A.D. 1100.

The Basketmakers built subterranean pithouse dwellings. These prehistoric structures were enclosed by walls made of vertical sticks, brush, and bunched grass. The roofs on the pithouses were supported by large beams and covered with smaller sticks and grass. Both the roofs and walls were finally coated with adobe mud and left to harden in the sun.

Opposite: Owachomo Bridge

Sometime after A.D. 700, the Basketmakers left the area, abandoning their mesatop structures. The Anasazi arrived several centuries later, attracted to the fertile land and flowing water here. They built small farming villages close to

intermittent streams and relied on both the retention and diversion of the valuable water from rain and snowfall each season. It was during this time that the people began to construct buildings on the surface of the ground—the pueblo dwellings and fieldhouses that are visible in the area today.

Nine-Mile Bridge View Drive is an auto loop that skirts the canyon's rim, providing spectacular views of the three natural bridges. Here are some highlights: From the Sipapu Bridge Overlook, Horsecollar Ruins can be clearly seen in a sandstone alcove across the canyon. A short but demanding hike from the Kachina Bridge Overlook leads to a well-preserved rock-art panel under the bridge. The remains of a prehistoric pithouse dwelling and granary are also tucked beneath the steep ledge at the end of this trail. A second trail meanders between Kachina Bridge and Sipapu Bridge and passes by the alcove holding Horsecollar Ruins, to the left.

The archaeological sites here are very fragile. Great care should be taken in and around these ruins, as the area holds significant spiritual meaning for contemporary Native Americans and are important links to native people of the past.

Horsecollar Ruins

I set up my tripod and camera in front of the buff-colored sandstone wall off to one side of Kachina Bridge and started to compose my images. A man and his wife were standing still as statues near the back of the overhang, their eyes fixed on the prehistoric handprints painted by ancient artists. Moments later the pair approached me. "What an interesting display," the man said as I looked up from under the dark hood of my large-format camera. "What do you think they mean?"

From our subsequent conversation, I learned that the couple was here from South Carolina, and that it was their eighth trip to the Southwest. Each year they pick a certain spot on the map, drive thousands of miles west, and, like early explorers driven onward by their sense of adventure and the thrill of new discovery, they hike and explore the canyons, cliffsides, and desert expanses where the ancient people lived.

Like so many visitors to the Southwest, including Cathie and me, once they'd set their eyes on the Four Corners region and felt the awesome presence of the people who explored and lived on this land thousands of years before, these travelers from the South were hooked. As they slowly walked toward the meandering creek that flows under Kachina Bridge, I wondered how many times they would return to the deserts of the Southwest, seeking solace, adventure, and answers to their questions about the ancient ones. Perhaps our paths would cross again someday, here in the red desert.

Ruins and rock art at Kachina Bridge

18 GRAND GULCH PRIMITIVE AREA

Bureau of Land Management
Grand Gulch Plateau
Recreation Management
435 N. Main St./P.O. Box 7
Monticello, UT 84535
(435) 587-1532

NEAREST SUPPLY CENTER:
Blanding, Utah

HIGHLIGHTS: **The Grand Gulch
Primitive Area, once home
to the Anasazi people and
the Basketmakers before
them, is a perfect destination
for those with a sense of
adventure. Ruins and artifacts
await your discovery!**

INTERPRETATION:
Self-guided tours

SEASONS OPEN: **All seasons**

HOURS OF OPERATION:
All hours

FEE AREA: **Yes**

ACCESS ROAD: **Paved**

DIRECTIONS: **The Grand Gulch
Primitive Area is just south
of Natural Bridges National
Monument, off UT 95. It is
managed by the BLM and
is accessible only by foot
or horseback. Permits are
required to hike and camp in
the area; contact the number
above for information.**

The steep canyon walls and deep washes at Grand Gulch seem inhospitable to human life, but they are testaments to the adaptability and survival skills of the Ancestral Puebloan (Anasazi) people who called this place home for centuries.

The Anasazi were not the first people to inhabit the canyon, however. Human remains of an ancient culture were found as the site was excavated, dating back as early as A.D. 200. These people became known as the Basketmakers due to their proclivity for the craft, and it was determined that they used different tools, wore different clothing, and were even slightly different in physical appearance than the Anasazi people who settled in the area roughly 800 years later.

Experts believe drought drove the Basketmakers to leave the site and many feel that the Anasazi people who returned to Grand Gulch around A.D. 1050 were descendents of this native race. Armed with superior farming techniques they had learned from the people of Mesa Verde to the east and the Kayenta people to the south, the Anasazi were able to farm this arid land successfully for centuries before leaving it behind for good.

Today, the vast area within Cedar Mesa remains one of our nation's richest sources of archaeological information. The cliffs and canyons contain easily accessible sites that beg for increased protection. Visitors can explore freely and discover beautifully preserved dwellings, rock-art panels, shards of pottery, and stone tools amid the sandstone walls here. With that privilege comes an equal amount of responsibility to leave artifacts where they lie and tread lightly through this archaeological wonder.

19 HOVENWEEP NATIONAL MONUMENT

McElmo Route
Cortez, CO 81321
(970) 562-4282

NEAREST SUPPLY CENTERS:
Cortez, Colorado, and
Bluff and Blanding, Utah

HIGHLIGHTS: Well-preserved
towers and pueblo structures
at Hovenweep National
Monument include six
different groups of ancient
structures, all situated on
tributaries of the San Juan
River. Four of these prehistoric
communities are in Colorado
and two are in Utah.

INTERPRETATION: Visitor center
and self-guided tours

SEASONS OPEN: All seasons

HOURS OF OPERATION:
All hours (visitor center is
open from 8 a.m. to 5 p.m.,
with extended summer hours.)

FEE AREA: Yes

ACCESS ROAD: Paved

DIRECTIONS: The monument
headquarters are at the
Square Tower site, which is
between White Mesa, Utah
and Cortez, Colorado. From
Cortez, take County Road G
(the McElmo Canyon Road)
west to the site. From White
Mesa, take UT 262 southeast
and follow the signs to the
monument. Stop at the visitor
center here for specific
directions to the remote
sites and hiking trails.

The earliest known report of Hovenweep Ruins was made by the leader of a Mormon expedition traveling through the region in 1854. Mr. W. D. Huntington spoke of the magnificent structures he saw and remarked at the ruggedness of the area surrounding them. Twenty years later, famed western photographer William H. Jackson captured this awe-inspiring area on film. It was Jackson who first called the area Hovenweep, a name he may have learned from the Paiute and Ute natives he met along his journeys through Utah and Colorado. Hovenweep, in the people's ancient language, means "deserted valley." In 1923, President Warren G. Harding called for the creation of Hovenweep National Monument and placed the historic area under the direction of the National Park Service for future generations to explore and enjoy.

Stronghold Tower, Twin Towers, Rim Rock House, Round Tower, Hovenweep House, Square Tower, Hovenweep Castle, and other smaller dwellings perch on the sandstone walls overlooking Little Ruin Canyon. In their prime, which was between A.D. 1100 and 1300, several of the towers were more than two stories high. These majestic structures have endured centuries of

Hovenweep Castle

natural weathering and erosion, and they stand today as tributes to the skilled Ancestral Puebloan (Anasazi) craftsman who designed and built them.

The ancient people who lived in the Hovenweep region were farmers and relied heavily on their unique understanding of the environment to feed their families. Water was paramount to their survival, and villages throughout the Hovenweep complex were built in close proximity to seeps and springs. The head of the drainage above Square Tower Ruins supports a thick grove of mature hackberry trees—a sign that the area contained enough moisture to nourish life in Little Ruin Canyon below.

On the sandstone rim above Square Tower, there is more evidence of the farming culture's ability to use precious moisture to its fullest. A series of check dams were put in place to hold seasonal runoff from snowmelt or rainfall. The collection pools either diverted water directly to the gardens and fields or allowed it to seep through the sandstone until it reached the bedrock layer below, where it ran along the impervious surface and flowed out of the cliff face. The ancient people who built these irrigation systems were experts at conserving and utilizing the natural elements that supported their agrarian way of life, and managing water in the semi-arid environment was particularly key to their survival.

Experts are uncertain as to the reason why the towers were built by ancient farmers. Though Tower Point sits at the head of two adjoining drainages and might have had some use as a watchtower, it does not seem as if these tall buildings were constructed for defense. Some experts believe the ancient farmers were expert celestial observers and charted the paths of the sun and stars. The small holes in the walls of many of the towers at Hovenweep seem to have been placed so that light from the setting sun would illuminate a certain spot on a tower's opposite wall. One alignment might take place on the exact date of the summer solstice and another on the date of the winter solstice. A third alignment would occur when the last rays of sunset glowed on the day of the equinox. By charting the position of the sun, the people were able to follow a yearly calendar of sorts, enabling them to read the seasons and plant and harvest their crops at peak times each year. Scholars believe the towers may have also served some sort of ceremonial role for the villages here.

Inexplicably, the ancient people of Hovenweep abandoned their stone dwellings within the canyons sometime after A.D. 1300, following the path of other San Juan inhabitants to Arizona and New Mexico. They left behind a legacy that instills a sense of wonder in visitors today.

The first, and perhaps most important, stop at the monument is the newly constructed visitor center, located just off the rim of Little Ruin Canyon. An easy, two-hour hike from here leads to a number of beautifully preserved and fascinating Anasazi towers and pueblo dwellings in the Square Tower Group. Directions to other sites within the monument—including Cajon, Hackberry, Holly, Horseshoe, and Cutthroat—are available at the visitor center.

Arizona

Wupatki National Monument;
Opposite: Kinishba Ruins;
Far right, top: Grand Canyon National Park;
Far right, bottom: Romero Ruins

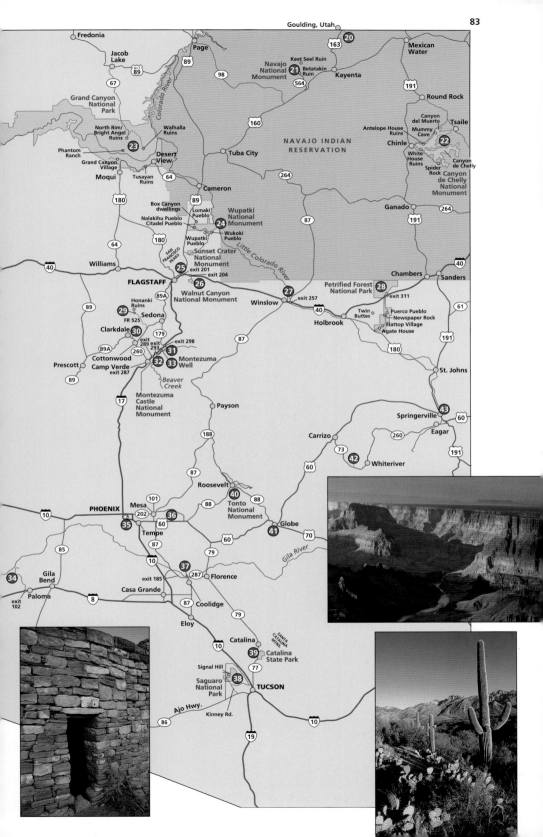

20 MONUMENT VALLEY NAVAJO TRIBAL PARK

Navajo Nation Parks and
Recreation Department
P.O. Box 2520
Window Rock, AZ 86515
(928) 871-6647

NEAREST SUPPLY CENTER:
Kayenta, Arizona (the small
town of Goulding, Utah, also
offers basic services)

HIGHLIGHTS: The Monument
Valley Navajo Tribal Park is
composed of 29,817 acres
within the Navajo Indian
Reservation. The visitor
center run by the Navajo
Nation often features native
artists at work, and the
guided tours are excellent.

INTERPRETATION: Visitor
center and guided tours

HOURS OF OPERATION:
May–September, 8 a.m. to
7 p.m.; October–April, 8 a.m.
to 5 p.m.

FEE AREA: Yes

ACCESS ROAD: Paved

DIRECTIONS: Monument Valley
Navajo Tribal Park is 22 miles
north of Kayenta, just one
mile off of US 163.

Mitchell Butte

During sunrise on most mornings, it's easy to see why Monument Valley is a sacred place to the Diné (Navajo). This semi-arid landscape is not actually a valley at all, but a broad, flat plain, 5,564 feet above sea level, punctuated by dry arroyos and towering buttes. The natural features in the park have attracted people to the area for thousands of years—from prehistoric migrants to the moviemakers, landscape photographers, and artists of today.

Before the arrival of the Diné, Paleo Indians roamed the area as long ago as 12,000 B.C. Archaic hunters followed sometime after 6000 B.C. in search of the meager resources available in the harsh desert environment. Little remains today to record the occupation of these early inhabitants because these nomads dwelled in temporary hunting camps

Sun's Eye

Raingod Mesa

and followed their prey from place to place. However, silent traces of these first people are apparent in the advancement of their more settled descendents.

The Ancestral Puebloan (Anasazi) people left the first clear record of human presence in Monument Valley. They established dwellings under cliff overhangs and in the open spaces between the sandstone towers. The most notable markings left by the Anasazi are their petroglyphs, which are found throughout the valley.

The Diné people now serve as the stewards of Monument Valley. Many of the park's guides grew up in the area and have heard the legends of Monument Valley from their elders. They lead tours to ruins and rock-art sites that are not open to the general public and share their knowledge of the history of this sacred place. The tours begin at the visitor center and last for a couple of hours.

Guides will share the legends behind the buttes and pinnacles of the valley, as many of these natural features have spiritual meaning to the Diné. The petroglyphs and ruins featured on the tours have also been studied extensively by the Navajo. They have made exciting discoveries about the relationship between the Anasazi people and their own and freely share their knowledge with visitors. These guided tours greatly help non-natives to gain a meaningful understanding of Native American customs, past and present.

An unguided visit to Monument Valley can also be a pleasurable experience. The 17-mile driving loop leads through one of the most beautiful landscapes to be found in the Southwest and gives visitors a close-up view of many spectacular buttes and dry washes. It is permissible to stop at a number of pullouts and overlooks along the route, but unguided hiking is not permitted. Some of the scenery might look familiar to you, as the buttes have served as the prominent backdrop for many Western epics such as *She Wore a Yellow Ribbon* and John Ford's classic *Stagecoach*.

Echo Cave Ruin

21 NAVAJO NATIONAL MONUMENT

HC-71, Box 3
Tonalea, AZ 86044-9704
(928) 672-2700

NEAREST SUPPLY CENTER:
Kayenta, Arizona

HIGHLIGHTS: The ruins at Keet Seel and Betatakin are very well preserved and offer a wonderful glimpse back into the everyday life of the Kayenta Anasazi— the village's most recent inhabitants.

INTERPRETATION: Visitor center, guided tours, and short, self-guided hikes (the monument is on the Navajo Indian Reservation, but it is under the management of the National Park Service)

SEASONS OPEN: All seasons

HOURS OF OPERATION:
8 a.m. to 5 p.m.

ACCESS ROAD: Paved

DIRECTIONS: The monument turnoff is 50 miles northeast of Tuba City and 22 miles southwest of Kayenta on US 160. A 9-mile road leads to the monument and visitor center.

The silent villages that remain under the sandstone alcoves inside Navajo National Monument are held in great reverence by the Navajo and Hopi people living in the Southwest. Artifacts uncovered in the archaeologically rich area chronicle almost 2,000 years of social development, extending from 750 B.C. to A.D. 1300, and experts believe the villages here once served as the hub of the northwest branch of the Ancestral Puebloan (Anasazi) culture.

The Anasazi people settled along the rich valley floors and hunted the bush-covered terrain and high mesatops for small game and edible plants. They also cultivated small fields near their village sites. Some experts believe the frequency of severe seasonal thunderstorms increased the natural occurrence of what is known as arroyo-cutting, or the repeated washing away of the fertile land along the narrow valley floors. This surface erosion presented a serious problem for the residents in the canyon, as it depleted the quantity of fertile land available for growing crops, placing great strain on the farmers and eventually forcing them to move from the valley. Scholars believe that, beginning in A.D. 1250, nearly half of the people living in the Tsegi Canyon area moved from their valley homes to sites in the cliffs above. The ancient people occupied these cliff dwellings for approximately 50 years before finally abandoning the area entirely and moving to land now occupied by the contemporary Hopi people.

Betatakin Ruins is one of the two most accessible cliff dwellings at Navajo National Monument and can also be viewed from an overlook at the visitor center. From May to September, the National Park Service provides ranger-guided tours to the ruins that take about five hours. The trail to Betatakin is strenuous but well worth the effort.

Final construction on the ruins we see at Betatakin today began around A.D. 1267. However, before the large pueblo structure was built, the location is thought have been used by prehistoric farmers as a seasonal camp. Experts also believe the alcove in which Betatakin Ruins now rests was probably first inhabited

Opposite: Betatakin Ruins

around A.D. 1260 by a small clan of Puebloan families acting as an advance party for the larger occupation that followed. Population at Betatakin Ruins peaked to 100 inhabitants sometime around the middle of the 1280s, but by A.D. 1300 the pueblo structures had been abandoned.

The walls remaining at Betatakin Ruins represent a distinct mixture of building styles. Most of the side walls were built using roughly prepared stones and thick layers of clay mud, which served as mortar. Many of the front walls making up the room blocks and storage spaces were constructed using a jacal-style construction, in which a framework of wood and brush was plastered with thick layers of mud. The physical layout of the pueblo at Betatakin Ruins allowed for the residential room blocks to face a large central plaza, where much of the daily activity within the village took place. The square kiva at Betatakin suggests that the outdoor plaza was also used for ceremonies and gatherings.

Keet Seel, the other large ruin site at Navajo National Monument, is even more remote. The eight-mile hike along the canyon rim and the descent of almost 1,000 feet to the canyon floor are not for the faint of heart, but the ruins and experience are well worth the journey. A trip to Keet Seel requires a backcountry permit, and access to the site can only be gained between May and September.

Scholars believe construction on the substantially larger ruins at Keet Seel began around A.D. 1250. The dwellings continued to grow with the population at Keet Seel, which almost tripled during the three-year period between A.D. 1272 and 1275, and experts believe construction ended at the site around A.D. 1286. At its peak, Keet Seel may have been home to as many as 150 residents. The site was abandoned around A.D. 1300.

The Keet Seel ruins include several distinctive features left behind by its builders, including a 180-foot retaining wall. Three wide walkways were laid out within the dwelling, accessing the long line of room blocks, kivas, and storage rooms. Large plazas or courtyards were built to provide both working and gathering space for the village inhabitants. In several rooms, and within the plaza areas, the Puebloan people set up rock-lined milling bins complete with large stone *metates*, or grinding tables, and grinding stones, known as *mano*. The granaries at Keet Seel were designed to keep out rodents and insects and consisted of crudely built jacal structures.

Keet Seel is considered to be one of the best-preserved ruin sites in the Southwest. A visual display of geology unfolds along the trail, and the journey gives visitors a timeless sense of what life must have been like in the canyon thousands of years ago.

22 CANYON DE CHELLY NATIONAL MONUMENT

P.O. Box 588
Chinle, AZ 86503
(928) 674-5500

NEAREST SUPPLY CENTER:
Chinle, Arizona

HIGHLIGHTS: The sheer sandstone walls of Canyon de Chelly and her sister canyons provide a dramatic setting for the relics of the indigenous people who called the area home.

INTERPRETATION: Visitor center, exhibits, self-guided tours, and Navajo-guided tours

SEASONS OPEN: All seasons

HOURS OF OPERATION:
The monument is open all hours; the visitor center is open from 8 a.m. to 6 p.m.

FEE AREA: No

ACCESS ROAD: Paved

DIRECTIONS: The monument, campground, and visitor center are 3 miles from the town of Chinle just off US 191.

White House Ruins

The breathtaking beauty of Canyon de Chelly and Canyon del Muerto, both situated within the national monument, is at times marred by the tragic history that lingers over the colorful cottonwood groves, red-sandstone cliffs, and silent pueblo ruins. The canyons were carved eons ago by the persistent flow of the Chinle Wash, which has watered the bottomlands here for thousands of years. It was the water that may have first attracted the early Basketmakers to Canyon de Chelly and Canyon del Muerto.

Between A.D. 300 and 420, sizable pithouse villages began to appear in the area surrounding the deep, slickrock canyons. During this period, the inhabitants of Canyon de Chelly and Canyon del Muerto relied on hunting game and gathering edible plants. By A.D. 550, however, they had come to depend more and more on domestic crops like corn, beans, and squash.

Gradually, the people began to look to the canyon bottoms and the floodplain as fertile ground for their fields. The Ancestral Puebloan (Anasazi) people moved

Spider Rock Overlook

from the canyon rims and outlying areas down to the flat ground below, though the plateaus around the canyons still remained occupied to some degree. Around A.D. 1050, the population in the entire region increased sharply as newcomers migrated to the area, and the villages here flourished.

Experts believe it was during this period of significant population increase that the pueblos seen today in Canyon de Chelly and Canyon del Muerto were constructed. Most of the larger villages were either built in hollow alcoves in the sandstone cliffs or up against the cliff walls at the edges of the canyons in order to be safe from seasonal flooding. As before, the rich ground at the bottom of the canyons was reserved for farming.

Despite the seeming success of their agriculture, the people of Canyon de Chelly and Canyon del Muerto gradually began to leave their pueblos and fields behind. Scholars believe that Mummy Cave, the last occupied site within the canyons, was abandoned by A.D. 1284, marking the end of a long legacy of Anasazi occupation here.

Nearly a century later, the Navajo, or Diné as they prefer to call themselves, began to migrate into the area of present-day Arizona, spreading across the new homeland they called Dinetah. Conflicts between the settlers and the Native Americans over land use and occupation of the area led to military action, first by the Spanish, in 1805, and then by the Americans in the 1860s. Complaints about Navajo hostility toward American settlers in Arizona and New Mexico led to the appointment of General James H. Carlton, who was charged with bringing the Diné to total submission.

Carlton employed the services of Kit Carson who, after chasing the native people through the canyons and across the mesas with little luck, took to setting

Antelope House Ruins

Rock art

their homeland on fire. Navajo homes, land, crops, and livestock burned in the wake of Carson's plot to starve the Diné into submission. Sick, hungry, and weak from the relentless chase, the Diné people fled to the sacred walls of Canyon de Chelly to defend their right to remain alive on their own homeland. The ground beneath the sandstone cliffs turned blood-red following the ensuing massacres, and the surviving Diné people were forced to surrender.

Thousands of Diné, including elders, children, and the injured, were forced to march 300 miles across Arizona and most of New Mexico to be incarcerated on a reservation on the Pecos River near Fort Sumner, New Mexico. For the next four years, death, disease, and starvation plagued the people. Thousands died at *Welde* (place of despair), and many contracted diseases. Finally, compassionate citizens of New Mexico intervened, and the government removed General Carlton from his post. In 1868, the Diné people were set free, and they walked once again over the 300-mile route that led back to Canyon de Chelly.

The site was designated a national monument on April 1, 1931 in order to honor and preserve its austere beauty and valuable history. Numerous rock-art panels serve as visual reminders of the extensive human occupation in the canyons and contain art from three distinct archaeological periods: Basketmaker, Pueblo, and Navajo. These paintings span centuries, featuring images reminiscent of ancient life, hunting, and ceremonial figures as well as the arrival of the Spanish conquistadors. Today, the Navajo Nation is the acting steward of Canyon de Chelly and Canyon del Muerto, which lie within the borders of the 16-million-acre Navajo reservation.

23 GRAND CANYON NATIONAL PARK

P.O. Box 129
Grand Canyon, AZ 86023
(928) 638-7888

NEAREST SUPPLY CENTER:
Williams, Arizona, on the
South Rim, and Jacob Lake
on the North Rim

HIGHLIGHTS: The natural
and cultural history of this
national park is truly grand!

LEVEL OF INTERPRETATION:
Visitor center, exhibits, and
self-guided tours

SEASONS OPEN: All seasons
on the South Rim; October
10–May 10 on the North Rim.
A call to the information line
of the National Park Service
(above) is recommended
before traveling to the
North Rim.

HOURS OF OPERATION:
All hours

FEE AREA: Yes

ACCESS ROAD: Paved

LOCATION: The South Rim
entrance is on AZ 64/US180,
57 miles north of its intersection with I-40 at Williams.
The North Rim entrance is at
the end of AZ 67, 44 miles
south of Jacob Lake.

The dramatic story of the Grand Canyon seems to unfold on the surface of its steep cliff faces. However, the layers of exposed rock merely outline the canyon's history. Archaeologists believe most of the landmass that made up the area around the present-day Grand Canyon has been swept away by wind and water erosion. Scattered rocks that towered above the ancient canyon millions of years ago now litter its floor.

The epic of the Grand Canyon extends back to the Paleozoic Era (roughly 550 to 250 million years ago), and the geological record here is gigantic in proportion to the record of human life within the canyon. Archaeologists believe the first humans arrived in the area as early as 4000 B.C. These desert nomads lived on wild plants and hunted animals. They camped for short periods of time, possibly seasonally, in caves or under large rock overhangs. Because of the

Tusayan Ruins

nomadic nature of the Archaic people, few traces of their presence remain within the Grand Canyon area today. However, split willow figurines in the forms of bighorn sheep and mule deer have been found and attributed to Archaic craftsmen. These fascinating fetishes are on display at the Tusayan Ruins.

Experts believe that sometime around A.D. 500 the Basketmaker people started to settle along the rims of the canyon and began cultivating their crops in the desert soil. Small villages were initially built along the South Rim, but within the next three centuries pithouse farming communities began to appear on the North Rim mesas as well. These subterranean dwellings were gradually replaced by pueblos.

The winter climate on both rims of the Grand Canyon can be brutal given the elevation and high winds that sweep through the area. To escape the harshness of winter and extend the growing season, some of the ancient farmers descended into the canyon and explored the far reaches of its shadowy gullies. By A.D. 1050, the Ancestral Puebloan (Anasazi) descendants of the Basketmakers were living and farming both in the canyon and on its rims.

Tusayan Ruins, just off South Rim Road between Desert View and Grand Canyon Village, has a small but very informative museum that is well worth visiting before you embark on the short walk to the ruins. Tusayan features the remains of a small pueblo structure as well as a sizable kiva adjacent to the residential site. Archaeologists believe both of these structures were built in the 1100s and were occupied for a short time. Fields were probably tended close to the ruin site, possibly in the open areas just beyond the kiva. There are a number of interpretive panels that provide insight into the lives of the 30 or so people who once inhabited the pueblo here.

Walhalla Ruins is on the North Rim near Walhalla Glades Overlook. The small pueblo structure is believed to have been occupied by a single family during prehistoric times. The people who lived here likely tended small gardenlike fields in the immediate area.

Bright Angel Ruins is one of the more remote sites found in the Grand Canyon. Like many of the ruins we see within the canyon today, this site was initially identified by John Wesley Powell during one of his two exploratory trips down the Colorado River beginning in 1869. The ruins are situated on the northern bank of the river and include evidence of early pithouses, probably occupied by a small group of residents around A.D. 1050. The remains of a small pueblo structure built around A.D. 1100 can also be seen here. Archaeologists believe the early inhabitants vacated their pithouse dwelling, but new inhabitants, attracted by the abundance of water and workable cropland, later moved to this site. They upgraded the dwellings and occupied the area for the next five or six decades before they themselves moved on.

A fairly strenuous hike of seven or nine miles (depending on the trail you choose) leads to the Bright Angel site. Due to the roughness of most canyon trails and the lack of water along the way, a fair amount of planning is necessary before heading out on the trails. However, the site is well worth the effort. A backcountry permit and reservation are required to camp in the area and can be obtained at Phantom Ranch.

Today, the far reaches of the Grand Canyon are occupied by the Southern Paiute people, who live on the North Rim, and the Havasupai, who reside and raise crops in the Havasu Creek area. These native people, along with the Hopi and the Zuni, who believe their people first ascended to this world from the depths of the Grand Canyon, consider the area to be a sacred place. In honor of these long-lasting beliefs, many native people return to the canyon to celebrate their spiritual heritage.

24 WUPATKI NATIONAL MONUMENT

Flagstaff Area National
Monuments—WUPA
6400 N. Highway 89
Flagstaff, AZ 86004
(928) 679-2365

NEAREST SUPPLY CENTER:
Flagstaff, Arizona

DESCRIPTION: The sites at Wupatki tell an epic story of more than 10,000 years of human occupation and cultural diversity representing Sinagua, Ancestral Puebloan, Hohokam, Mogollon, and Cohonina people.

INTERPRETATION: Visitor center and self-guided tour (access to the public ruins is via well-maintained trails, with almost no off-trail exploration allowed)

SEASONS OPEN: All seasons

HOURS OF OPERATION: Spring and fall, 8 a.m. to 5 p.m.; summer, 8 a.m. to 6 p.m.; winter, 9 a.m. to 5 p.m.

FEE AREA: Yes

ACCESS ROAD: Paved

DIRECTIONS: Wupatki National Monument lies between the towns of Flagstaff and Cameron, on US 89. A 36-mile loop road passes through Sunset Crater and Wupatki National Monuments. Entrances for the loop are well marked and are 12 miles and 26 miles from Flagstaff, respectively.

Nalakihu Pueblo

Wupatki National Monument occupies 56 square miles of rugged high-desert terrain and contains more than 2,000 archaeological sites ranging from single-room, prehistoric field-houses to the huge, 100-room Wupatki Pueblo. The geographic region around the monument and nearby Verde Valley has been called a cultural melting pot—a melting pot in the midst of an environment seemingly unsuitable for the long-term occupation of humankind. The Navajo people believe that the San Francisco Peaks, or *Dook' o' sliid* (Light Shines From It), mark the western border of their native lands, and both the Hopi and Zuni trace ancestral ties back to the sacred ground within the boundaries of Wupatki National Monument.

The first humans probably arrived in the area around the Little Colorado River and San Francisco Peaks as early as 11,000 years ago. This theory was based on the discovery of a Clovis point dating back to Paleo Indians who roamed the region. However, these people were nomadic, and little record of their presence here remains.

A number of primitive pithouse dwellings and work sites dating back to A.D. 500 and attributed to Archaic people are the first record of settlement in

Opposite: Lomaki Pueblo

Wupatki Pueblo

Wupatki Pueblo
Below: Nalakihu Pueblo

the area. As human occupation here continued, the people began to farm the land, using whatever moisture was available to irrigate their fields. They built fieldhouses near their small plots of corn, beans, and squash, and their crops began to spread across the semi-arid landscape.

Industrious farmers, the Sinagua people, so named by archaeologists for their ability to live with very little water, captured seasonal rain and snowmelt and diverted water from small springs through a series of check dams and irrigation ditches and onto their fields. The Sinagua survived in their high-desert environment for more than 400 years until the volcanic cone, now known as Sunset Crater, began to shake the landscape. Alerted to coming events, the

Sinagua temporarily left the area around the San Francisco Peaks. The cone erupted from A.D. 1064 to 1065, darkening the sky with black ash, hot cinders, and poisonous gas which would have probably destroyed the Sinagua had they not departed for safer ground. Molten lava flows covered the landscape, killing all of the plant and animal life in the area. The thick, black ash spread for 800 square miles from the point of eruption, collecting on the ground like a blackened snowfall.

After the eruption, the Sinagua moved back into the area of Wupatki and began to settle in again. They cultivated crops, greatly aided by the mineral-rich ash left by the eruption. A very favorable climate change brought more rain to their fields as well, and the population around the area of the San Francisco Peaks and Little Colorado River grew significantly.

Experts believe the Kayenta Anasazi people migrating from the north began to settle in the region, soon to be joined by Winslow Anasazi from the east and Cohonina from the west. The Hohokam and Mogollon people may have also migrated here from their homelands in the south. These different cultures quickly blended with the Sinagua, and the new community began to construct the impressive pueblo villages scattered today across the landscape of Wupatki National Monument.

A short, clearly marked spur road leads to **Wukoki Pueblo.** This impressive site offers a less crowded experience than Wupatki. Citadel Pueblo, Nalakihu Pueblo, Box Canyon dwellings, and Lomaki Pueblo are on the north end of the loop road heading back to US 89. These sites offer wonderful photographic opportunities with the San Francisco Peaks in the background.

Wupatki Pueblo

Wukoki Pueblo

25 ELDEN PUEBLO

Coconino National Forest
Peaks Ranger Station
5075 N. Highway 89
Flagstaff, AZ 86004
(928) 526-0866

NEAREST SUPPLY CENTER:
Flagstaff, Arizona

HIGHLIGHTS: This unique site
has hands-on archaeological
experiences for the public
through programs such as
Family Excavation Week
and Public Dig Days (see
information below).

INTERPRETATION:
The Coconino National Forest
has established and presently
manages an archaeological
program at Elden Pueblo
that allows individuals and
groups to participate in
excavations at the site. For
more information, contact
The Elden Pueblo Project,
Arizona Natural History
Association, P.O. Box 3496,
Flagstaff, AZ 86003;
(928) 526-0866.

SEASONS OPEN: All seasons

HOURS OF OPERATION:
All hours

FEE AREA: No

ACCESS ROAD: Paved

DIRECTIONS: Elden Pueblo
is just outside Flagstaff on
US 89, 1.5 miles north of its
intersection with I-40. The
entrance to the ruins is on
the west side of the road
and is clearly marked.

In 1926, under the sponsorship of the Smithsonian Institution, archaeologists Jesse Walter Fewkes and John P. Harrington partially excavated the ruins at Elden Pueblo. Their research helped to define what experts know today as the Elden Phase of the Sinagua culture. The name Sinagua is a combination of two Spanish words—*sin* meaning "without" and *agua* which means "water"—that define the people and their struggling lifestyle.

The Sinagua were believed to have first arrived in the region sometime around A.D. 500. Unfortunately, due to the eruption of the Sunset Crater in A.D. 1064 and 1065, much of the archaeological record of the early Sinagua here was lost forever; their pithouses remain entombed beneath thick layers of ash and cinder. As a result, most of the artifacts and structural remains uncovered by contemporary researchers date back to the people who returned to the area after these eruptions and built pueblo dwellings.

Elden Pueblo was occupied between A.D. 1150 and 1275 and may have housed as many as 300 people at its peak. The village probably included a small number of self-contained pueblo structures and rooms, and as more inhabitants moved into the area additional structures were built. When the final stage of construction was complete, many of the original units were joined together to form a large pueblo.

A great community room and the sizable ceremonial kiva were two of the last structures added to the complex. These buildings suggest that Elden Pueblo was important to the other communities throughout the area and may have been used for gatherings or trade. Although many of the villages in this region were well populated, few structures designed for large-scale community use have been found.

Elden Pueblo, like many archaeological sites found in the San Francisco Peaks area, is also considered sacred to the Hopi people. The site is believed to have been a place where the Hopi ancestors lived for a period of time during their long migration and search for a sacred homeland in this world.

26 WALNUT CANYON NATIONAL MONUMENT

Flagstaff Area National
Monuments—WACA
6400 N. Highway 89
Flagstaff, AZ 86004
(928) 526-3367

NEAREST SUPPLY CENTER:
Flagstaff, Arizona

HIGHLIGHTS: Walnut Canyon
is known for its distinctive
Sinagua ruins as well as
its unique and beautiful
natural environment.

INTERPRETATION: Museum
and self-guided tours
(guided hikes are available
with advance reservations
from Memorial Day to
Labor Day)

SEASONS OPEN: All seasons

HOURS OF OPERATION: Spring
and fall, 8 a.m. to 5 p.m.;
summer, 8 a.m. to 6 p.m.;
winter, 9 a.m. to 5 p.m.

FEE AREA: Yes

ACCESS ROAD: Paved

DIRECTIONS: Head east on
I-40 from Flagstaff for 7 miles
to the Walnut Canyon
exit (204). The monument
is 3 miles south of the exit.

In the 1880s, the Smithsonian Institution dispatched James Stephenson to examine the cliff dwellings in Walnut Canyon. He was followed by Jesse W. Fewkes, a familiar name to archaeology in the red-rock regions of Arizona. Though the site was designated a National Monument in 1915, little was done to protect the antiquities of Walnut Canyon from the greedy pursuits of pot-hunters, and the ruins within the canyon were all but destroyed by looting and general disregard. In 1993, as a result of the hard work and dedicated efforts of many Arizona citizens, the ruins received the protection they deserved.

The prehistoric Sinagua people inhabited the pueblos tucked within the limestone walls of Walnut Canyon some 800 years ago. The name Sinagua is taken from a pair of Spanish words: *sin* meaning without and *agua* meaning water. True to their name, the industrious people forged a living in the deep, dry ravines and dense forests of Walnut Canyon and thrived within the seemingly inhospitable and arid landscape.

The Sinagua are believed to have been Walnut Canyon's only permanent inhabitants. They began to build pithouse communities in the dense forests atop the canyon's rim as early as A.D. 600. A survey of the north and south rims identified 214 archaeological sites, including garden terraces, small fieldhouses, and a number of pueblolike structures.

The prehistoric people hunted for game, gathered the abundant plants that thrived on the forest floor, and began to cultivate domestic crops. They captured the seasonal rainfall and snowmelt with crudely constructed check dams along the forest floor's drainages and diverted this water onto small gardens planted with corn, squash, and beans. As the size of their fields increased, collecting and retaining water, as well as precious soil, became increasingly important.

In roughly A.D. 1064, the Sunset Crater volcanic area grew more active, finally erupting and spreading a thick covering of black ash and cinder across the region. The catastrophic nature of this event could have eradicated the people of Walnut Canyon, but the Sinagua seem to have had warning of the eruption and moved away during this tumultuous time.

When the Sinagua returned to Walnut Canyon, their agriculture blossomed. The volcanic material that covered the ground may have increased the fertility of the land around the region, making it better suited for farming, and the annual rainfall in the area seems to have increased greatly, making agriculture a less risky enterprise. It is also possible that they learned new techniques from other farming cultures while they were away. In any event, the Sinagua culture flourished between A.D. 1065 and 1200, and the people built the cliff dwellings we see today, tucked within the deep alcoves in the limestone cliffs above the canyon floor.

It seems that as quickly as good fortune set in, however, it also disappeared. By A.D. 1250, the cliff dwellings and terraced fields in and around Walnut Canyon had been abandoned, this time for good. The Sinagua people are believed to have relocated to the high mesas southwest of Flagstaff, in the present-day homeland of the Hopi.

27 HOMOL'OVI RUINS STATE PARK

HCR 63, Box 5
Winslow, AZ 86047
(928) 289-4106

NEAREST SUPPLY CENTER:
Winslow, Arizona

HIGHLIGHTS: The ruins, rock-art panels, ceremonial sites, and sacred sanctuaries at Homol'ovi Ruins serve as testaments to the spiritual value of the land and the ingenuity of the people who once settled here.

INTERPRETATION: Visitor center and self-guided tours

SEASONS OPEN: All seasons

HOURS OF OPERATION:
All hours

FEE AREA: Yes

ACCESS ROAD: Paved

DIRECTIONS: From I-40 just east of Winslow, take Exit 257 and proceed north on AZ 87. The park is approximately 1.5 miles from the exit.

Potsherds

The migration of the ancient nomads across the Southwest was, at least in part, an epic journey to find their sacred homeland. The ancestral people built villages along the way and left physical traces of their remarkable lifestyle behind. These sites, and the paintings and artifacts that remain in them, are sacred to the Hopi people who descended from this prehistoric race.

According to experts, the Ancestral Puebloan (Anasazi) people first arrived in the Homol'ovi area sometime around A.D. 750 and lived in small pithouse villages close to their fields. Along with their crops, the ancient people gathered wild food including agave, prickly pear, amaranth, mesquite beans, and bee-weed. They also took advantage of the host of wild game attracted to the area by the lush, green environment along the banks of the Little Colorado River.

The primitive pithouse dwellings here were abandoned due to changes in the climate throughout the arid regions of the desert Southwest, and the farmers migrated to areas better suited to their agriculture. However, sometime after A.D. 1000, the farmers returned to the banks of the Little Colorado River, this time to establish several large pueblo villages.

By A.D. 1200, experts believe an entirely new group of people had flooded into the area, significantly expanding the population around Homol'ovi. Larger pueblos were built in order to accommodate the growing community—Homol'ovi I was made up of approximately 250 rooms while Homol'ovi II may have contained as many as 1,000 rooms—and cultivated fields sprang up all along the floodplain of the Little Colorado.

In addition to corn, beans, and squash, the people also began to grow cotton, which they used as a raw trade commodity and to make their beautiful textiles. Trade was an important element of the growing Homol'ovi culture, and the central location of this pueblo allowed its inhabitants to exchange goods with people in villages to the north and south. Trade goods such as shells brought in from as far away as Mexico and the coast of California, pottery originating in the Verde Valley, and tools and ornamental artifacts of Hohokam, Sinagua, and Mogollon origin have all been uncovered at Homol'ovi. The diversity of goods and artifacts found during the excavation here demonstrates the wide radius of the prehistoric trade network, which was active for centuries. Many experts believe it was this industrious interaction that caused the Homol'ovi culture to advance rapidly during the early years.

Experts are uncertain as to why, but by the early 1400s the people of Homol'ovi began to abandon the huge pueblos they built along the river and continued their path of migration. Perhaps a hint as to the reason can be derived from the rock art left behind. One of the more dominant geometric figures, repeated in the ancient rock art throughout the Southwest, is the spiral. There are those within contemporary Hopi culture who believe the spiral symbolizes the continued migration of their ancestors as they searched for their true homeland. The outward flow of the spiral signifies the long journey, beginning from within the interior of the earth and leading to the Hopi Mesas where the people finally settled and remained. For the Hopi, there is great meaning in each of the elements of their long journey through the spiral of life. Homol'ovi was one curve in the spiral and thus shaped the Hopi people of today.

Homol'ovi Ruins

28 PETRIFIED FOREST NATIONAL PARK

P.O. Box 2217
Petrified Forest
National Park, AZ 86028
(928) 524-6228

NEAREST SUPPLY CENTER:
Holbrook, Arizona

HIGHLIGHTS: The Petrified
Forest area is rich with
natural and human history.
Petrified trees, pueblo ruins,
and rock-art sites provide
vivid glimpses of the past
in this unique place.

INTERPRETATION: Visitor center
and self-guided tours

SEASONS OPEN: All seasons

HOURS OF OPERATION: 8 a.m.
to 5 p.m. (call for extended
hours during the summer)

FEE AREA: Yes

ACCESS ROAD: Paved

DIRECTIONS: Entrances to the
park can be found 25 miles
northeast of Holbrook on
I-40 and 19 miles east of
Holbrook on US 180.

The saga of the landscape around present-day Petrified Forest National Park begins during a time geologists refer to as the late Triassic Period, 208 to 245 million years ago. Retreating oceans and heavy erosion produced a floodplain that was carved and molded over time by a vast number of silt-bearing streams with thickly wooded banks. As the banks eroded under the increasing force of the waters, the tall trees fell, were swept downstream, and came to rest in the deep, sticky mud covering the floodplain. Silt soon finished the job of entombment, depriving the saturated logs of oxygen and slowing their rate of decay. In this environment, silica-rich minerals gradually replaced the normal wood fiber, and, over the eons, the logs began to crystallize into quartz. This colorful timber graces the landscape of Petrified Forest National Park.

There is also an epic story of human life upon this land. People have inhabited this area continuously for the last 10,000 years. Both Hopi and Navajo legends recall the presence of the petrified trees, cast like shadows across the desert landscape. An ancient Navajo story holds that the logs scattered across the ground were once the bones of a giant, Yietso, slain by the Diné's primal ancestors who first arrived on the surface of the new world. A traditional story told by the Hopi suggests that the petrified trees are the remains of huge arrow shafts launched by the ancient thunder god, Shinuav.

Scholars believe the Archaic people were among the first to make use of the hardened quartz by flecking sharp tools and weapons from the glassy material. Unfortunately, little evidence of the Archaic people remains within the borders

of the park due to their nomadic lifestyle. They probably visited the area on a seasonal basis and never established permanent camps from which their customs could be traced.

The ancient hunters were replaced by a long line of more advanced societies such as the Ancestral Puebloan (Anasazi). Research in the area has identified more than 300 archaeological sites attributed to the Anasazi, ranging from simple field shelters and rock-art panels to complex pueblo structures containing as many as 75 rooms.

Flattop Village lies in the southern portion of Petrified Forest National Park and consists of approximately 25 prehistoric pithouse structures scattered across a remote section of land. The subterranean dwellings were lined with sandstone slabs, and the walls and roofs were surfaced with a mat of juniper sticks and brush coated with bulky layers of mud. These cool desert dwellings were accessed by narrow entryways at ground level. The partially excavated ruin site at Flattop Village is one of the oldest studied sites within the park.

Twin Butte, occupied between A.D. 500 and 800, is made up of 15 individual pithouse complexes built adjacent to one another. Archaeologists believe each unit may have served as a home for an extended family or clan. Unlike the Flattop Village site, the dwellings at Twin Buttes were entered through small hatchways in the roof. These entryways also provided ventilation for the subterranean dwellings by working in tandem with holes and air deflectors near the hearth.

Puerco Ruins

The partial excavation of the Twin Butte site revealed that trade was an important aspect of life for the people here. Nearly half of the pottery uncovered at the site was actually produced by the neighboring Mogollon culture. It is conceivable the residents of Twin Buttes traded petrified wood for the Mogollon Brownware found in shards here.

Agate House is an eight-room pueblo structure built on the top of a small hill in the area now called Rainbow Forest. This site was occupied from A.D. 1000 to 1300. The surface dwelling was originally built from blocks and slabs of petrified wood held in place by thick layers of clay mortar.

Puerco Pueblo served as a home for two separate groups of ancient people. Experts believe the pueblo was first occupied in A.D. 1000 and remained in use for a century before it was inexplicably abandoned. A devastating drought plagued the Southwest in the first part of the 1200s. Lack of moisture forced the people living in scattered communities throughout the area to relocate to villages closer to reliable sources of flowing water. One group of people migrated to the banks of the Puerco River and moved into an empty pueblo located there.

The village, which may have housed a farming community of 60 or 70 residents from A.D. 1300 to 1400,

Newspaper Rock

contained several rooms arranged around a central plaza. A number of ceremonial kivas were constructed within the pueblo, suggesting an increased interest in spirituality. Perhaps the people were hoping to appeal to the rain gods for compassion during the long drought. In any event, the riparian location of Puerco Pueblo probably allowed the Anasazi to remain in the area for up to a century longer than they would have been able to endure the drought conditions at their previous village.

Two of the hundreds of rock-art sites in the Petrified Forest area are close to Puerco Ruins. The cliff face on the east side of the river near the ruins is a good place to view petroglyphs, as is Newspaper Rock (above), which is just down the road from the ruins site.

29 PALATKI CULTURAL HERITAGE SITE AND HONANKI RUINS

Coconino National Forest
Red Rock Ranger District
250 Brewer Rd.
Sedona, AZ 86336
(928) 282-4119

NEAREST SUPPLY CENTER:
Sedona, Arizona

HIGHLIGHTS: The Palatki
Cultural Heritage Site is
under the jurisdiction of the
U.S. Forest Service and offers
guided tours of the ruins
and rock art in the area.

INTERPRETATION:
Guided tours

SEASONS OPEN: All seasons

HOURS OF OPERATION: 9:30
a.m. to 7:30 p.m., 7 days a
week (subject to weather
conditions). Reservations
are required.

FEE AREA: Yes

ACCESS ROAD: Gravel

DIRECTIONS: From downtown
Sedona, drive 7 miles west
on AZ 89A until reaching
FR 525. Turn right and then
proceed 6 miles north to a
sign for Palatki. Continue
for another 2 miles to the
visitor center and parking
lot. Directions to Honanki
Ruins can be obtained at
the Palatki visitor center.

The name Palatki is from the Hopi language and, loosely translated, means "red house." Jesse W. Fewkes chose the name for this site in 1895 during his archaeological studies within the Verde Valley region.

The pueblo ruins at **Palatki** consist of two separate structures probably occupied by at least two groups of Sinagua people. Data obtained through tree-ring analysis and pottery shards suggests that both pueblo structures were built between A.D. 1130 and 1280. Experts believe that, at the peak of their occupancy, the two pueblos at Palatki Ruins may have housed between 30 and 50 people from the same family or clan. The large, white, shieldlike pictograph above the eastern pueblo may have been a clan symbol, possibly identifying the specific group or family that occupied the area. The western ruins appear to have been the smaller of the two but include a kiva that may have served as a gathering place for the village residents.

Opposite: Palatki Ruins

The area around the Palatki Ruins is also well known for the ancient rock-art panels across the ravine from the ruin sites. The trail to these panels begins to the west of the visitor center and winds its way along the base of the overhanging cliffs with deep alcoves carved out by erosion. Some of the best-preserved pictographs and petroglyphs to be found within the Verde Valley area are tucked inside these alcoves. The rock art here depicts the occupation of indigenous people from Archaic hunter/gatherers to the more recent Yavapai and Apache people.

The pictographs are painted in a variety of colors, each made from natural pigments. The white pigment was made from kaolin clay, the red tint from pulverized hematite, and the yellow tincture was made from powered limonite. The distinctive black color featured on many of the more contemporary art samples at the site is charcoal.

The first alcove along the trail is known as **The Grotto** and includes rock art specimens ranging from Archaic times to A.D. 600. Continuing along the trail you will come to Bear Alcove, named for the three bear figures sketched in charcoal high on the wall. The image of figures mounted on horses helped experts trace the latter years of occupation to more contemporary tribes, as the horse was not introduced to this part of the Southwest until the late 1500s.

Palatki Ruins

Roasting Pit Alcove hosts a collection of prehistoric rock-art features including a resting Kokopelli, the ancient flute player. Directly in front of this alcove is the unexcavated roasting pit that gives this site its name. It was used by the Sinagua to cook agave plants, a staple food for the ancient people of the Verde Valley. Some experts believe the Sinagua left the settlement at Palatki in some haste, because the large pit seems to contain the roasted remains of the last agave harvest.

Honanki Ruins lie several miles past Palatki. Visitors are encouraged to obtain information at the Palatki visitor center before embarking on a trip to Honanki Ruins, as the roads are often impassable after a heavy rain or snow.

The name Honanki is from the Hopi language and means "bear

house." Scholars believe that what is now Honanki Ruins was one of the more populated areas in the Verde Valley during ancient times. The ruins, situated in an alcove, include a 60-room pueblo occupied by the Sinagua sometime between A.D. 1130 and 1300. Like the Palatki site, Honanki also contains a number of pictograph and petroglyph panels, most of which have never been scientifically studied. Artifacts associated with Archaic nomads, Southern Sinagua, Yavapai, and Apache people, as well as rock-art images depicting the passage of early Anglo pioneers, have all been discovered at this site.

Archaeologists believe the Sinagua abandoned the ruins at Palatki and Honanki prior to A.D. 1300 and may have migrated to larger pueblos in the area like Tuzigoot or the Cornville group. The Hopi people of today hold the area around Palatki and Honanki very sacred and return on a frequent basis to hold ceremonies and to honor their forefathers. The walls of Honanki Ruins are extremely fragile, so please use great care when exploring this site.

30 TUZIGOOT NATIONAL MONUMENT

Tuzigoot Road
Clarkdale, AZ 86324
(928) 634-5564

NEAREST SUPPLY CENTER:
Clarkdale, Arizona

HIGHLIGHTS: Tuzigoot
National Monument is one
of the places from which the
industrious Sinagua culture
grew. The ruins that remain
here today speak to the
advanced nature of this
desert-dwelling society.

INTERPRETATION: Visitor center
and self-guided tours

SEASONS OPEN: All seasons

HOURS OF OPERATION:
Summer, 8 a.m. to 6 p.m.;
winter, 8 a.m. to 5 p.m.

FEE AREA: Yes

ACCESS ROAD: Paved

DIRECTIONS: Tuzigoot
National Monument is
located on AZ 89A midway
between Cottonwood and
Clarkdale. The turnoff to
the monument is clearly
marked and easy to find.
A short road leads from
the turnoff to the parking
lot and visitor center.

The ruins at Tuzigoot National Monument are perched on a small hill overlooking the lush banks of the Verde River. Two trails, each a quarter-mile in length, lead visitors through the area, which is managed by the National Park Service.

The name Tuzigoot is of Apache origin and means "crooked water." The village was once home to the people whom experts now call the Southern Branch of the Sinagua. Scholars who have studied the Sinagua believe they descended from the ancient Hohokam, developing a distinct culture of their own over the centuries. As Sinagua villages grew larger and more successful, migrating visitors from the north, such as Ancestral Puebloans (Anasazi) and perhaps even the Mogollons, probably influenced the Sinagua culture.

The residents of Tuzigoot were kin to the Northern Branch of the Sinagua, who settled in the mountainous regions close to the San Francisco Peaks and north of the present-day Verde Valley. They were thought to have arrived in the region around A.D. 500. At first, the Southern Sinagua built subterranean pit-house dwellings situated reasonably close to their small croplands. As their culture grew and became more agriculturally based, the people built larger and more complex dwellings. Pueblos like the one found at Tuzigoot sprang up throughout the Verde Valley during this prosperous time, around A.D. 700.

From a distance, the re-stabilized ruins appear to tuck themselves into the landscape. The stone room blocks seem to amble from their perch on the 150-foot knoll down toward the valley floor, following the natural contour of the hillside like an outgrowth of the hill itself. This is due to the unique pattern of the colorful walls of Tuzigoot, which do not match up with one another, giving them a zigzag appearance that blends with the hillside.

The first phase of construction at Tuzigoot began around A.D. 1000 with a series of 12 small rooms near the top of the knoll. Sometime around A.D. 1200, the second construction phase began, adding complementary room blocks. By A.D. 1300, the third and last phase of construction was well under way, producing the collection of structures that remain today. When the Tuzigoot pueblo was complete, it contained as many as 77 individual ground-floor rooms along with a central plaza. The two-story pueblo served as a home for approximately 200 Sinagua people.

The thick walls at Tuzigoot were built from limestone and sandstone from the area. Layers of rock were held together by red-clay mortar and chinked with smaller stones, strengthening the structure by increasing the tightness of the chinking. The Sinagua also built support structures within the walls in order to suspend the huge wooden beams that made the framework for the roof. Thatch composed of cottonwood, juniper, sycamore, and piñon material was laid across the beams.

The Sinagua were industrious farmers and worked the bottomland surrounding their pueblo for generations. They also hunted small and large game in the fields, hillsides, and marshy areas around the village. Mule deer, pronghorn, rabbits, ducks, turtles, and geese were part of the Sinagua diet. Mesquite beans, yucca, cactus, walnuts, acorns, and cattails were also used for food as well as for medicinal purposes. Agave, roasted in large, stone-lined pits, supplemented the people's diet, particularly when other food was scarce.

Despite the fertile fields and natural abundance surrounding the Tuzigoot village, the structures were abandoned by A.D. 1425. The Sinagua are thought to have migrated east to the Chavez Pass area and finally to the pueblo village of Homol'ovi on the Little Colorado River, near the town of Winslow, but the reason for their departure remains a mystery.

31 V-BAR-V RANCH PETROGLYPH SITE

Coconino National Forest
Red Rock Ranger District
250 Brewer Road
Sedona, AZ 86336
(928) 282-4119

NEAREST SUPPLY CENTER:
Sedona, Arizona

HIGHLIGHTS: The V-Bar-V
Ranch Petroglyph Site is in
a beautiful setting along
Beaver Creek, surrounded
by deciduous trees and open
meadows. The sandstone
cliffs here are adorned with
more than 1,030 petroglyphs
left by the Sinagua people.

INTERPRETATION:
Guided tours

SEASONS OPEN: All seasons

HOURS OF OPERATION:
Monday–Friday, 9:30 a.m.
to 4:30 p.m. (the entrance
gate closes at 3:30 p.m.)

FEE AREA: Yes

ACCESS ROAD: Paved

DIRECTIONS: V-Bar-V Ranch
Petroglyph Site is 3 miles
south of the intersection of
I-17 and AZ 179, south of
Sedona. At Exit 298, proceed
south on AZ 179 for about
3.5 miles to the sign and
gate for V-Bar-V. There is
a nice campground along
Beaver Creek on the way
to the site.

Sometime around A.D. 1400 the climate in
the Verde Valley began to change and temper-
atures rose. The Sinagua farmers were forced to
relocate to larger communities housing as many
as 100 inhabitants. In these ancient villages,
valuable resources including water and manpower could be consolidated in a
more efficient manner, giving residents more time to pursue artistic endeavors.
One of these communities was situated atop the hill overlooking Beaver Creek,
directly above what is known today as the V-Bar-V Ranch Petroglyph Site.

Experts believe the valley around Beaver Creek may have served as a primary
trade route for the ancient people of the greater Verde Valley. Perhaps the
petroglyphs along Beaver Creek were meant to attract the attention of those
who passed by, possibly serving to direct travelers to the village above.
Regardless of its original purpose, this area hosts one of the most informative and
photogenic rock-art displays in the Southwest.

Studies at a number of similar sites have led scholars to believe the petroglyphs at V-Bar-V Ranch were probably created sometime between A.D. 1150 and 1400. Due to the consistency of artistic style that flows across the panels, and given the even degree of weathering present at the site, experts believe the petroglyphs were probably created by the same group of artists over an extended period of time. This is somewhat unusual, as most rock-art panels span several time periods and represent a variety of styles and even distinct cultures. (A good example of this diversity exists nearby at the cliffs of Palatki Ruins, where the art includes Sinagua, Apache, and Yavapai images all on the same walls.)

The Sinagua art at V-Bar-V includes a variety of human figures as well as zoomorphic images of coyotes, turtles, lizards, and cougars. The paintings of cranelike birds here represent some of the sharpest images of their kind to be found in the Southwest. Bear paws also decorate the walls at V-Bar-V. Bears were considered by many prehistoric people to possess spiritually important qualities, and they are often the subject of myths and legends passed down through oral tradition. Perhaps the paws here are the work of Sinagua shamans as they prayed for fruitful crops, successful hunts, or the health of their people.

An interesting element of the petroglyphs at V-Bar-V is the pairing of similar images. Pairs of turtles, women, and sticklike humans adorn the walls. None of the images physically overlap; however, a few seem to be connected to one another by meandering lines or arms.

The V-Bar-V petroglyphs were protected by the owners of the V-Bar-V Ranch for many years before the site was acquired by the U.S. Forest Service. As a result, the images were saved from vandalism and are in remarkable condition today. Even the trees that shade the petroglyphs seem to be hiding them in an effort to keep the rock art as pristine as possible for future generations to enjoy.

32 MONTEZUMA CASTLE NATIONAL MONUMENT

2800 Montezuma Castle Rd.
Camp Verde, AZ 86322
(928) 567-3322

NEAREST SUPPLY CENTER:
Camp Verde, Arizona

HIGHLIGHTS: This large and impressive cliff dwelling is one of the most accessible and best-preserved sites in the region. Its architectural integrity is a testament to the skill and ingenuity of the Sinagua culture.

INTERPRETATION: Visitor center and self-guided tours

SEASONS OPEN: All seasons

HOURS OF OPERATION:
Memorial Day–Labor Day, 8 a.m. to 7 p.m.; otherwise, 8 a.m. to 5 p.m.

FEE AREA: Yes

ACCESS ROAD: Paved

DIRECTIONS: The site is 50 miles south of Flagstaff off I-17. Take Exit 298, just north of Camp Verde. Look for signs to the national monument.

The stately cliff dwellings at Montezuma Castle National Monument are believed to have been occupied by the Southern Branch of the Sinagua people. The largest and most impressive dwelling at the site, Montezuma Castle is tucked within a deep alcove carved on the face of the tall limestone escarpment by millions of years of erosion.

Below the huge cliff face, the waters of Beaver Creek have created a mineral-rich basin that supports beautiful groves of sycamore trees and a thick mat of underbrush. The lush bottomlands attracted wild game and the hillsides and meadows adjacent to the basin supported a varied assortment of wild plants. The favorable climate, as well as a long growing season and mineral-rich soil, made the Verde Valley particularly well suited to a farming culture.

Experts believe that prehistoric people first arrived in the area between A.D. 500 and 600. Through years of social development, the Sinagua split into two distinct groups; the Northern Branch remained in the mountain country around the San Francisco Peaks while the Southern Branch migrated farther south into what is known today as the Verde Valley.

By A.D. 700, the Southern Sinagua were well established in the valley and living in pithouse farming villages. The dwellings were dug into the ground and lined with flat stones and clay plaster. The pithouse walls and roof were supported by timbers covered with smaller poles, brush, and thick grass, then coated with a thick layer of mud and clay that hardened in the desert sun.

Over the next century, the pithouse villages in the Verde Valley increased in size, and surface pueblos began to appear. Farmland was at a premium and many of the fields were a considerable distance from the villages. In order to tend these remote plots, individual farmers built thousands of small, pueblo-style fieldhouses, which they occupied until the minerals in the soil were depleted. The farmers moved around the valley in search of fertile ground, and more and more fieldhouses began to dot the landscape.

As the centuries unfolded, the Southern Sinagua culture thrived. Already successful as both a farming culture and a trading society, the ancient Sinagua followed a social trend apparent throughout the Southwest: They moved from their outlying farms to more centralized communities. Large pueblos were constructed along many of the major tributaries of the Verde River in cliff faces or atop the ridges of mesas. Substantial masonry structures like Montezuma Castle sprung up throughout the region and bustled with activity.

Construction of Montezuma Castle began in about A.D. 1100. The stone walls were built from blocks of limestone gathered from the floor of the alcove or hauled up the cliff face from below the dwelling site. The blocks were secured with thick clay mortar and were plastered or surfaced with adobe mud. The exterior walls were constructed close to the edge of the cliff and were two feet thick at the base, tapering to one foot at their highest level. The south-facing walls retained heat from the low angle of the sun during the winter months yet stood in cool shade during the hot summer, making the stone structure comfortable year-round. The roof is supported by large sycamore beams, probably cut along Beaver Creek and transported up the steep cliff.

The interior of Montezuma Castle is divided into smaller rooms that have been preserved over the years by the dry environment and the large cliff overhang above the dwelling. Entry was gained through hatchways built in the roof, and residents navigated the levels of the castle on a series of interior ladders. The rooms inside were accessed by small doorways, some of which are T-shaped like

those found in Ancestral Puebloan villages of Mesa Verde and Chaco Canyon. The alcove itself was likely accessed by long ladders that stretched up the cliff face from its base below. Montezuma Castle probably housed about 50 people, but it is believed to have been abandoned after a brief occupancy.

A second pueblo site, known as Castle A, lies a short distance up the paved path from the cliff dwelling. Castle A is the remains of a five-story pueblo situated against the base of the overhanging cliff. Unfortunately, this site was damaged almost beyond repair by vandals and pothunters, and there is little that remains of the original structure today.

Montezuma Castle

33 MONTEZUMA WELL

2800 Montezuma Castle Rd.
Camp Verde, AZ 86322
(928) 567-3322

NEAREST SUPPLY CENTER:
Camp Verde, Arizona

HIGHLIGHTS: Montezuma Well
is under the jurisdiction of
Montezuma Castle National
Monument. Although the
well itself—actually a sinkhole fed by underground
springs—is breathtaking,
the steep limestone cliffs of
its uppermost edge also
hide the pueblo ruins of a
prehistoric culture.

INTERPRETATION:
Self-guided tour

SEASONS OPEN: All seasons

HOURS OF OPERATION:
Memorial Day–Labor Day
8 a.m. to 7 p.m.; otherwise
8 a.m. to 5 p.m.

FEE AREA: No

ACCESS ROAD: Paved

DIRECTIONS: Montezuma
Well is 50 miles south of
Flagstaff, off I-17. Take Exit
298 and head south on
AZ 179. The route is clearly
marked and always well
maintained.

Millions of years ago, a huge, bubblelike dome made of calcium carbonate formed over the mouth of a mineral-rich hot spring deep below the surface of the earth. The dome expanded for thousands of years, pushing up against the limestone above it. Once enough pressure had built up, the dome collapsed to form a gigantic sinkhole measuring 470 feet in diameter. The prehistoric sinkhole is constantly fed by underground springs and must have been a welcome oasis in the desert for the first nomadic people who arrived here.

The Hohokam people, the original residents at Montezuma Well, are thought to have arrived sometime after A.D. 600 and probably remained in the area for an extended period of time. One of their pithouse dwellings, believed to have been occupied around A.D. 1100, is open for viewing and can be found along the road that leads from the parking lot to the gate at the monument entrance.

The Sinagua people, believed to be the descendants of the Hohokam, built cliff dwellings along the narrow overhangs on the interior edges of the sinkhole, and these well-preserved structures remain today. Other Sinagua ruins are found throughout the area and range in size from single-room field shelters to the 55-room pueblo at the well site. Approximately 150 to 200 Sinagua people are thought to have lived near Montezuma Well between A.D. 1125 and 1400.

During the Sinagua occupation, experts believe the village at Montezuma Well may have served as a gathering place for inhabitants of the Verde Valley. Some believe the significant growth in trade that took place during the time of the Sinagua occupation may be due to the strategic location of several villages including the one at Montezuma Well. The collection of artifacts recovered at the site includes items that arrived in the valley via trade with indigenous people living in the far reaches to the north and south. Shells from the Gulf of Mexico and the coast of California, as well as crimson macaw feathers from the interior regions of Mexico, have been uncovered at several Verde Valley sites. The discovery of these artifacts demonstrates just how far the prehistoric trade networks reached during the time of the Sinagua. Similarly, Sinagua art and craft objects, including fine, woven textiles, have been uncovered in excavations in the far reaches of the Southwest.

A cement walkway winds its way along the upper rim of the limestone sinkhole. A trail also departs the edge of the rim, descends to the well below, and follows along the bank before coming to a dead end at what appears to be a prehistoric storage room. Another trail leads to the discharge end of the well where examples of the ancient irrigation canals can be found. The springs feeding the well are rich in lime and other minerals, and deposits still coat the remains of the old irrigation canals.

The site is sacred to the contemporary Hopi people who, through legends and traditions, trace their ancestors back to the area. Little is known about the spiritual significance of Montezuma Well. However, the oral tradition of the Hopi people holds valuable history about their ancient connection to this lovely and wondrous place.

34 PAINTED ROCKS PETROGLYPH SITE

Bureau of Land Management
Phoenix Field Office
21605 N. 7th Ave.
Phoenix, AZ 85027
(623) 580-5500

NEAREST SUPPLY CENTER:
Gila Bend, Arizona

HIGHLIGHTS: Painted Rocks
Petroglyph Site boasts one
of the Southwest's most
concentrated collections
of prehistoric petroglyphs.

INTERPRETATION:
Information panels

SEASONS OPEN: All seasons

HOURS OF OPERATION:
All hours

FEE AREA: Yes

ACCESS ROAD: Paved

DIRECTIONS: Traveling west on
I-8 from Gila Bend, proceed
13 miles to the Painted Rocks
exit (102). Follow the paved
road north for another
10 miles to the entrance,
and follow the signs to
the petroglyph site.

Painted Rocks Petroglyph Site (formerly known as Painted Rocks State Park) is believed to contain more than 700 individual petroglyphs. Many of the beautiful rock-art images are thought to have been the work of the Hohokam people who lived in the Gila Bend region from around A.D. 300 to 1450. The site also includes a number of rock-art figures chiseled by the more recent indigenous inhabitants to the area, including the Pima and Papago people.

The park is managed and protected by the Bureau of Land Management, which has successfully stopped the vandalism and theft that plagued the area before it was put under protection and given on-site management.

Several of the dark boulders at the Painted Rocks site are covered with petroglyph images, inviting close examination. The artists chose these dark rocks for their patina, or desert varnish, which, when chipped away, contrasted with the lighter rock beneath. The rock art here displays both geometric forms and zoomorphic images of the natural world around the ancient artisans. Serpents, lizards, birds and a variety of mammals gleam brightly from the rocks at the site. The Hohokam people also seemed to have a particular talent for depicting anthropomorphic forms. Images of humans flying or connected by holding hands circle the rims of Hohokam pottery vessels and rock-art panels.

The site also includes the more contemporary work of the Pima and Papago people. These images—from the maze of prehistoric patterns and symbols to Christian crosses and more contemporary depictions—display the time periods spanned by the native people's occupation here.

We may never fully understand the reason why ancient people selected places like Painted Rocks to display their complex rock-art storyboards. Maybe the outcrop was a landmark amidst the barren landscape or a vantage point for the indigenous people who traversed the area. Or, perhaps they marked the rocks to tell a small segment of the story of their existence within the parched wilderness. The location may have also been powerful or sacred in some way to the ancient people. We may never know.

The intended meaning behind much of the art at Painted Rocks is also a mystery to archaeologists. However, there are some within contemporary Native American society who, through the knowledge passed to them by the generations before, retain the ability to interpret the petroglyphs on their ancestral homeland. It is from these invaluable sources that today's archaeologists have gathered clues that help us understand, to some degree, the incredible display of images here.

35 PUEBLO GRANDE MUSEUM AND ARCHAEOLOGICAL PARK

4619 E. Washington St.
Phoenix, AZ 85034
(602) 495-0901

NEAREST SUPPLY CENTER:
Phoenix, Arizona

HIGHLIGHTS: This site, which is managed by the city of Phoenix, is a great place to learn about the history and architecture of the Hohokam people and to experience the exciting discoveries of archaeology.

INTERPRETATION: Museum, guided tours, and self-guided exploration

SEASONS OPEN: All seasons

HOURS OF OPERATION:
Monday–Saturday, 9 a.m. to 4:45 p.m.; Sunday, 1 p.m. to 4:45 p.m.

FEE AREA: Yes

ACCESS ROAD: Paved

DIRECTIONS: From I-10 in Phoenix, take the 48th Street exit northbound to Washington Street and continue to the museum, at the intersection of Washington and 44th Streets.

The Hohokam people lived and prospered in the pueblo village known today as Pueblo Grande for more than 1,500 years. Their innovative use of irrigation systems to water their crops, including corn, beans, and squash, enabled these farmers to sustain their large community. At its peak, Pueblo Grande was home to more than 1,000 inhabitants, and the village may have stretched as far as two miles across the desert. Now, much of the ruins lie beneath the city of Phoenix, but several features remain for public view.

As early as A.D. 750, the Hohokam began to divert the water of the Salt and Gila rivers to nurture their farmland. Over the years, their extensive system of canals reached farther and farther from the Salt River, and some experts believe this irrigation network provided water for more than 16 Hohokam villages. Some of the fields irrigated by the Salt River were as far as 10 miles from the river.

Despite their agricultural development, the ancient people continued to gather natural foods and herbs and to hunt game to supplement their diet. Many experts believe the prehistoric people domesticated turkeys, using the meat for food and the feathers for making blankets and clothing.

The ruins at Pueblo Grande include a large earthen mound that was constructed above a complex of pueblo structures. A number of residential, ceremonial, and storage rooms were built atop the mound, which is approximately 150 feet by 300 feet on its topmost surface. This surface was tightly sealed with a thick coating of mud tempered with a cementlike *caliche* and allowed to harden in the desert sun.

The mound contains a staggering 720,000 cubic feet of fill material such as rock, rubble, and desert soil thought to have been hauled to the site in baskets carried by Hohokam laborers. It is hard to imagine that such a huge earthen form was built without the use of modern-day machinery. However, when it came to engineering accomplishments, the Hohokam people always seemed to excel.

Similar platform mounds have been found in as many as 50 Hohokam sites throughout the deserts of Arizona. These mounds are especially common along the primary drainage of the Salt and Gila Rivers, where extensive irrigation systems were also utilized. While the purpose of the mounds remains unclear, most of them offer unimpaired views of the extensive irrigation systems. Perhaps these mounds served as lookouts from which the ruling class could manage the work in the fields below.

The ruins and canals at Pueblo Grande stand as testaments to the engineering mastery and agricultural skill of the Hohokam people, who were able to cultivate crops and develop their culture for centuries in the midst of the harsh desert.

36 PARK OF THE CANALS

1710 N. Horne St.
Mesa, AZ 85203
(480) 644-2351

NEAREST SUPPLY CENTER:
Mesa, Arizona

HIGHLIGHTS: The ancient canals that remain at Park of the Canals, now a city park, are testaments to the ingenuity of the Hohokam farmers.

INTERPRETATION:
Information panels

SEASONS OPEN: All seasons

HOURS OF OPERATION:
8 a.m. to 10 p.m.

FEE AREA: No

ACCESS ROAD: Paved

DIRECTIONS: Park of the Canals sits between McKellips Road and Brown Street, two of the main thoroughfares in Mesa. From AZ 202, take the McKellips Road exit and then proceed to Country Club Road. Turn right, continue to Horne Street, and turn left.

The Hohokam people who once inhabited the regions around Mesa, Arizona, were known both as masters of desert farming and as accomplished artisans. Scholars believe that Hohokam farmers began to use elaborate irrigation systems to supply water to their fields as early as A.D. 300. However, it was at least another 300 years before ancient farmers migrated into areas along the tributaries of the Gila and Salt Rivers, where they began to master the highly developed irrigation techniques that allowed their culture to flourish for generations. The Park of the Canals is one of the only places left within the land of the Hohokam where a modern visitor can view the remains of these ancient canals.

It is hard to imagine just how a culture of ancient people armed with tools no more sophisticated than stone hoes, wooden digging sticks, and large baskets could have built such an advanced system of irrigation. The intricate network of canals began with check dams or rock piles placed in the river to divert the flowing water through head gates and into the canals. These narrow canals were carved deeply into the ground to reduce surface evaporation. The larger canals dispersed into a series of smaller ones before the water finally poured onto the cultivated fields.

In 1878, a small party of settlers looking for suitable farmland for their families arrived in the area around Lehi, Arizona. They were told by others living in the area that no land was available in the valley. Their only option existed atop the mesas rising to the south. The group pushed onward toward the mesas and upon their arrival found thousands of unsettled and fertile acres of beautiful land. As the group explored the mesa more carefully, they discovered evidence of what appeared to be an ancient system of canals built by a people who thrived upon the rich land centuries ago.

Excited by the prospects before them, the party devised a plan to put the ancient canals back into use and create productive farmland for their families. The men set to work, using the remains of the canal system as a base. Aided by a common straight edge and a spirit level, the new builders searched for a place to put a new head gate for the revitalized irrigation system. The place they chose was less than two miles from the spot where the ancient Hohokam farmers had placed theirs.

After seeking the assistance of a U.S. government surveyor, the settlers were quickly informed that their plan to bring water to the mesa area by way of gravity flow would be impossible, because it appeared the irrigation water would have to flow uphill for a fair distance. But the settlers believed in the ingenuity of the ancient people. The party approached the surveyor once again and pleaded for a further investigation of the matter. As it turned out, the surveyor found that the water could, in fact, flow to the high mesas by the force of gravity alone if the head gate were moved approximately 100 feet. By April 1878, water soaked the ground atop the mesa once again, and new inhabitants began to harvest food from the fertile land.

Remains of an ancient irrigation canal

37 CASA GRANDE RUINS NATIONAL MONUMENT

1100 Ruins Dr.
Coolidge, AZ 85228
(928) 723-3172

NEAREST SUPPLY CENTER:
Coolidge, Arizona

HIGHLIGHTS: Casa Grande
Ruins National Monument was
our nation's first federally
protected monument. The
park includes a number of
Hohokam structures believed
to have been built around
A.D. 1300 as well as remnants
of their ancient irrigation
system.

INTERPRETATION: Visitor center,
museum, and self-guided tours

SEASONS OPEN: All

HOURS OF OPERATION:
8 a.m. to 5 p.m.

FEE AREA: Yes

ACCESS ROAD: Paved

DIRECTIONS: The monument
is between Phoenix and
Tucson, just off AZ 87/287
north of Coolidge.

Casa Grande ruins

The Hohokam people are believed to have migrated into the tributary areas around the Gila and Salt Rivers between A.D. 550 and A.D. 900. Initially, they occupied small villages within the region, but as their population grew and their farming efforts expanded, the Hohokam began to cluster into larger, more centralized communities like the site found at Casa Grande. Some scholars believed this was an intentional effort made by the industrious farmers to conserve land and to use resources, including manpower, more efficiently. Together, these farmers excavated narrow irrigation canals from the Gila River to their fields, and the remains of these waterways can still be seen here today.

The structures at Casa Grande include a number of well-preserved residential room blocks and a large ball court of sorts. The court was surfaced with hard-packed *caliche*—a mixture of clinch (mineral-rich dirt high in calcium carbonate) and water, which takes on the consistency of modern-day concrete when dry. Some experts believe the ball games played here may have been used to settle minor disputes between differing social factions. Others believe the games held a spiritual or ceremonial significance, or they may simply have been a display of the Hohokam's playful nature. The ancient ball court at Casa Grande is one of more than 200 found throughout the Southwest today.

However, it is the Great House, standing erect on an otherwise flat desert landscape, that gives this site its name. The spectacular red walls of this pueblo can be seen from far across the desert and drew visitors to the site long after the Hohokam had left. The Papago and Pima were the first to call the massive adobe structure *hottai-ki* or Great House. These indigenous people were followed by Spanish missionaries and explorers, and later by U.S. soldiers, federal archaeologists, and National Park Service stewards.

Archaeologists have studied the Great House extensively, attempting to uncover its hidden past. The structure appears to have been built in a single phase by a host of workers, using the ancient architectural techniques seen at other Hohokam great houses throughout the Southwest. The imposing edifice is four stories high with adobe-style walls up to four feet thick.

Ponderosa pine, mesquite, white fir, and juniper served as roofing material for the tall structure and often lined the interior floors. Experts believe there were as many as 640 12-foot beams used in the construction of the Great House as well. A portion of the wood was gathered in the mountains and hauled to the site by Hohokam porters, some of whom may have carried the huge timbers for 50 or 60 miles.

The purpose of the Great House remains unclear. There are those who maintain that the stately building was nothing more than a large storage silo used to hold excess crops. Others say the structure was home to Hohokam rulers and enabled them to monitor the irrigation system and direct the social and economic activities of the village from above. A growing field of thought now supports the possibility that the massive structure was used as an astronomical observatory or celestial calendar. During the summer solstice, light from the setting sun shines through one of the rounded openings in the upper walls of the Great House, and the beam is framed perfectly by the windows on the opposite side of the room, providing a visual sign that the solstice has arrived.

Although they thrived for generations in the harsh and unforgiving environment, by A.D. 1450 the Hohokam had virtually disappeared from the Southwest. Archaeologists speculate that crop failure due to drought, flooding, or insect plagues could be responsible for the people's departure, but the true reason for their migration remains, like many things at Casa Grande, a mystery.

38 SAGUARO NATIONAL PARK WEST

Saguaro National Park
Tucson Mountain District
2700 N. Kinney Rd.
Tucson, AZ 85743
(520) 733-5158

NEAREST SUPPLY CENTER:
Tucson, Arizona

HIGHLIGHTS: Set against the rugged Tucson Mountains, Saguaro National Park's West District is an explorer's paradise. The landscape is punctuated by the park's namesake cacti, but a closer look will reveal traces of the people who made their homes here in ancient times.

INTERPRETATION: Interpretive panels and self-guided hikes

SEASONS OPEN: All seasons

HOURS OF OPERATION: Park, 7 a.m. to sunset; visitor center, 8 a.m. to 5 p.m.

FEE AREA: Yes

ACCESS ROAD: Paved

DIRECTIONS: From I-10 in Tucson, go west on AZ 86 (the Ajo Hwy.). Proceed to Kinney Road and turn right. Follow the signs to the visitor center.

Spring Hill petroglyphs

The Hohokam people are believed to have occupied Sonoran Desert regions from as early as 300 B.C. to A.D. 1400. The early Hohokam constructed pithouses or jacal huts—dwellings in which the walls and roof rose from a floor dug approximately three feet into the ground. These subterranean structures themselves developed in style over the centuries, and, in the later period of Hohokam occupation in the area, the desert farmers began to build pueblos similar to those found at sites throughout the Southwest.

As their life in the Sonoran Desert developed, the Hohokam became more and more dependent on crops they grew in irrigated gardens and fields. The agricultural lifestyle left the Hohokam with leisure time, which they spent crafting pottery, jewelry, and art.

The evolution of Hohokam pottery styles and rock-art designs gives archaeologists a sense of the development of the Hohokam culture as a whole. Traces of the people's ancient origins come to the surface as their art is studied in detail, and these artifacts have led some experts to believe that the Hohokam may have had an ancestral connection to Mesoamerican cultures.

Signal Hill, one of the most popular rock-art sites, lies along Hohokam Road just above its namesake picnic ground. A half-mile hike leads across a dry wash and ascends a narrow path marked by a series of information panels. As you climb the gradual hillside, look for a collection of prehistoric petroglyphs on the rocks above. Artists used sharp stone tools to peck images on the dark surface of these rocks, which had taken on a patina, or desert varnish, over time. The chiseled images exposed the lighter rock beneath, and, thousands of years later, these petroglyphs still gleam brightly against the dark surface.

A number of trails within Saguaro National Park West lead to more remote ruins and rock-art sites once frequented by the prehistoric Hohokam people. It

is the policy of the National Park Service not to identify the specific location of these remote sites, so hidden signs of ancient Hohokam culture await your discovery as you explore the trails here. Please remember to leave artifacts in place for others to enjoy.

39 ROMERO RUINS

Catalina State Park
P.O. Box 36986
Tucson, AZ 85740
(520) 628-5798

Santa Catalina Ranger District (direct contact for the ruins): (520) 749-8700

NEAREST SUPPLY CENTER: Tucson, Arizona

HIGHLIGHTS: Romero Ruins, located in Catalina State Park, is a site full of natural beauty and cultural intrigue.

INTERPRETATION: Information panels

SEASONS OPEN: All seasons

HOURS OF OPERATION: Park, 5 a.m. to 10 p.m.; visitor center, 8 a.m. to 5 p.m.

FEE AREA: Yes

ACCESS ROAD: Paved

DIRECTIONS: Romero Ruins is located inside Catalina State Park, 10 miles north of Tucson on AZ 77 (Oracle Road). The Romero Ruins Interpretive Trail is just a short distance from Sutherland Wash picnic area, not far from the park entrance.

Saguaro cactus

The rugged Santa Catalina Mountains serve as a breathtaking backdrop for Romero Ruins. The ancient pueblo site here is neither restored nor completely visible, but it is adequately marked with panels that provide detailed information about the structures and the lifestyle of the Hohokam farmers who first established the community at Romero.

The Hohokam people are believed to have occupied the site between A.D. 500 and A.D. 1450, and as many as 300 inhabitants may have lived in the village at its peak, which probably occurred sometime after A.D. 850. The ruins we see here today outline a village composed of mostly subterranean structures. Large pits, approximately three feet deep, were dug in the ground. Walls extended upward from the pits and consisted of a siding of thin poles, sticks, and brush coated with thick, gummy layers of mud and desert clay that hardened in the intense desert sun. The walls were spanned by thatched roofs made from reeds, brush, and grass and supported by mesquite beams or other dense wood gathered in the area. This hutlike structure is known today as a jacal.

The Hohokam village at Romero Ruins, most of which is still buried below the grassy mounds, once thrived because of the consistent flow of water that streamed through Sutherland Wash. The water came from a source high in the mountains and flowed far enough below the hilltop so as not to pose a threat to the dwellings during the raging floods common to the area. However, the ancient farmers had to protect their terraced gardens and fields from the effects of spring runoff and flash floods. They built check dams and diversion ditches to channel the water onto their fields when needed and away from them when flooding endangered the crops.

The fertile land and the rough mountains and foothills in the region also provided habitat for a host of wild animals. The ancient people hunted with throwing sticks, bows and arrows, and snares woven from yucca fibers. The people tanned the hides of mule deer and bighorn sheep and used the leather to make a variety of household articles and clothing. Animal bones, sinew, and hooves were crafted into tools and weapons.

The remains of two ball courts at Romero Ruins are similar to those found at other Hohokam sites throughout the Southwest. Archaeologists wonder about the cultural importance of these oblong depressions. Some scholars feel the games played on these courts spawned from ceremonial rituals. Others believe that the Hohokam's theory of origin, from worlds far below the surface of the earth, might have had something to do with the role of the subterranean courts. Perhaps future studies at this site will reveal the answer!

40 TONTO NATIONAL MONUMENT

HC02 Box 4602
Roosevelt, AZ 85545
(928) 467-2241

NEAREST SUPPLY CENTER:
Roosevelt, Arizona

HIGHLIGHTS: The cliff
dwellings at Tonto National
Monument, accessed by a
short hike or guided tour,
provide a glimpse back in
time to the world of the
Salado people.

INTERPRETATION: Visitor
center, museum, guided
tours, and self-guided
adventures. Guided tours
of the Upper Ruins are
available November–April;
reservations are required.

SEASONS OPEN: All seasons

HOURS OF OPERATION:
8 a.m. to 5 p.m.

FEE AREA: Yes

ACCESS ROAD: Paved

DIRECTIONS: Tonto National
Monument is on AZ 88,
30 miles northwest of Globe
and just east of the small
town of Roosevelt.

Tonto National Monument was first established in 1907 by President Theodore Roosevelt. However, during the first 26 years of its monument status, the 640-acre preserve received little in the way of protection. Fortunately, the site was placed under the stewardship of the National Park Service in 1937, and its borders were expanded to include a total of 1,120 acres.

The abundance of water probably attracted the Hohokam to this area around A.D. 850. These people were accomplished desert farmers in the Salt River's fertile floodplain and employed extensive irrigation systems to bring water to their crops. Staples such as corn, beans, cotton, squash, and pumpkins thrived in the nitrogen-rich soil. The Hohokam also enjoyed a dependable supply of wild game and native plants from the steep sides of the broad basin. It was not long before the population grew and villages stretched from one end of the basin to the other.

For almost 300 years the Hohokam culture in the Tonto Basin remained intact. As time went on, however, the strong social traditions began to disappear, and by A.D. 1150 a new culture of people known as the Salado (after the Rio Salado, or Salt River) had evolved. Some experts believe this change was the result of the steady influence of the Ancestral Puebloan (Anasazi) people from the north or even the Mogollon culture to the east. Others believe the Hohokam were actually replaced over time by a new group of migrating people.

Over years of cultural transition, the Salado grew to become accomplished artisans, producing one of the most striking pottery styles found anywhere in the Southwest. Salado women used clay dug from areas along the Salt River and tempered it with sand washed from the rugged landscape around the basin. Their art is now referred to as Tonto Polychrome, and the jars, bowls, and figurines are known for their rich color and design.

Among the many questions experts have about the lives of prehistoric people in the Southwest is why a farming culture dependent on rich soil and plentiful water would suddenly relocate to the mountains, as the Salado people did. Could it have been the threat of marauding nomadic tribes moving through the area? Or was it social unrest within their own society that caused the people to leave their homes in the lowlands and move to the cliffs far from their fields? Archaeologists hope to discover clues to help solve this mystery.

Two ruin sites are open to visitors at Tonto National Monument. The **Lower Cliff Dwelling** is found at the end of a one-mile trail that winds its way through the high desert environment directly above the park's visitor center. The **Upper Cliff Dwelling** is a significantly larger structure and includes 32 rooms on the ground floor and eight second-story rooms. This site can only be viewed on a ranger-guided tour, and reservations should be made in advance.

41 BESH-BA-GOWAH ARCHAEOLOGICAL PARK

Jesse Hayes Rd.
Globe, AZ 85501
(928) 425-0320

NEAREST SUPPLY CENTER:
Globe, Arizona

HIGHLIGHTS: The large pueblo structures at Besh-Ba-Gowah reflect the evolution of the Hohokam culture as the people expanded outward from their ancestral homeland in the Salt and Gila River basins.

INTERPRETATION:
Interpretive panels, museum, and self-guided tours

SEASONS OPEN: All seasons

HOURS OF OPERATION:
9 a.m. to 5 p.m.

FEE AREA: Yes

ACCESS ROAD: Paved

DIRECTIONS: The town of Globe is 87 miles east of Phoenix. Approaching Globe on US 60, take the Broad Street exit and turn right when it intersects with Jesse Hayes Road. The Besh-Ba-Gowah site is clearly marked at this intersection; just follow the signs to the park.

The Apache term Besh-Ba-Gowah, or "place of metal," refers to the plentiful amount of copper found in the area. The mineral was first mined here in the 1870s, and there are still active mines in the region today. The Hohokam, who originally settled along the rich floodplain in the Salt and Gila River basins, migrated and formed new communities, like the one at Besh-Ba-Gowah, to take advantage of the untouched, fertile land and tributaries of the great rivers.

Scientists believe Pinal Creek and many of the smaller tributaries flowed year-round during prehistoric times. The inhabitants of these areas benefited from the constant flow of water, the temperate climate, and the long growing season found here. The abundant moisture also sustained native plants that diversified the people's diet. Descendants of nomadic hunters, the Hohokam also continued to rely on wild game for food. They hunted mule deer, bighorn sheep, and rabbits in the mountainous regions and brush country around Besh-Ba-Gowah. Hides, antlers, and animal bones were crafted into clothing, tools, and weapons.

During early excavations at Besh-Ba-Gowah, primitive Hohokam pithouses were found underneath the pueblo's rooms. This discovery proved to experts that, prior to the construction of the impressive Salado pueblos here, the Hohokam maintained a sizable population dating back as early as A.D. 550. Researchers believe the prehistoric people first settled in smaller villages along Pinal Creek, farming and hunting in the remote regions around the present-day pueblo. At some point, the Hohokam began to centralize their dwellings into larger hamlets, perhaps to consolidate their land and labor resources, and the ancient community flourished.

The migration of the Hohokam people into tributary areas like Pinal Creek marked the gradual decline of their cultural identity. It appears that the farther the Hohokam got from the vast basins along the Salt and Gila Rivers, the more affected they were by the traditions and beliefs of other native people. After generations of this social influence, the Hohokam culture seemed to dissolve and was replaced by what is now known as the Salado.

Sometime around A.D. 1225, the Salado people began constructing the buildings that remain in ruins today. At its peak, the large pueblo village consisted of approximately 146 ground-level rooms and more than 60 second-story rooms on top of the original pithouses. The residential rooms faced a number of open plazas where most of the daily activities, including cooking, grinding corn and other food items, and some ceremonies, took place. A fair number of rooms at Besh-Ba-Gowah were also set aside for storing crops.

The well-preserved pueblos at Besh-Ba-Gowah are prime examples of cross-cultural development and also indicate the importance of trade to the early people of the Southwest. Scholars believe the Salado builders were influenced by the Ancestral Puebloans (Anasazi), living to the north, and the highly successful Mogollons, to the east. Some experts have even found traces of ancient Mesoamerican culture at the site. Jewelry that was recovered during excavations at Besh-Ba-Gowah demonstrate the people's reliance on an extensive trade network that once reached as far away as Mexico.

42 KINISHBA RUINS

White Mountain Apache
Cultural Center and Museum
P.O. Box 507
Fort Apache, AZ 85926
(928) 338-4625

NEAREST SUPPLY CENTER:
Whiteriver, Arizona

HIGHLIGHTS: Kinishba Ruins
is a less-traveled site and
provides visitors with a
glimpse of both excavated
and untouched Pueblo ruins.

INTERPRETATION: The site
itself has no interpretation,
but the White Mountain
Apache Cultural Center and
Museum provides information
and interpretive displays.

SEASONS OPEN: All seasons

HOURS OF OPERATION:
Monday–Friday, 8 a.m. to
5 p.m.; summer Saturdays,
8 a.m. to 5 p.m.

FEE AREA: Yes

ACCESS ROAD: Gravel, which
may be impassable after
heavy rains

DIRECTIONS: Kinishba Ruins
is off AZ 73, 15 miles west
of Whiteriver. The turnoff
for the ruins is well marked
and is followed by 4 miles
of gravel road. Please stop
at the cultural center before
proceeding to the ruins.

The Kinishba Ruins sit in the 1.7-million-acre Fort Apache Indian Reservation and are presently under the stewardship of the Apache people. The name Kinishba is believed to have come from the old Apache language and means "brown house."

The first recorded account of the prehistoric structures at Kinishba came from the pen of famed anthropologist Adolph Bandelier in the 1880s. Much of the early excavation and research was done from 1931 to 1939 by a group from the University of Arizona led by archaeologist Bryon Cummings. The party excavated and partially restored the southeastern section of the ruin and cataloged a sizable collection of precious artifacts.

The large Ancestral Puebloan (Anasazi) settlement at Kinishba is believed to have been built and occupied between A.D. 1250 and 1400. However, a sizable pithouse village discovered beneath one of the pueblos dates human occupation back to the Basketmaker period, from A.D. 500 to 750. At one point in time, as many as 1,500 to 2,000 inhabitants may have lived at the site, and the ancient village may have contained as many as 600 individual rooms during the peak of its occupancy, around A.D. 1325.

Some of the masonry walls at Kinishba stood three stories high. The large room blocks were built around central plazas that served as gathering places. Spiritual ceremonies and rituals may also have been performed in these open courts in an effort to bring abundant rain and successful harvests to the village.

The people of Kinishba traded with their close neighbors as well as those living great distances from the Whiteriver region, and the archaeological record here shows a great deal of Hohokam, Sinagua, Mogollon, and Kayenta Anasazi influence. As a result, the site is important to our understanding of the cross-cultural relationships between the ancient people of the Southwest. Recently, thanks to the stewardship and dedication of the Apache Nation, Kinishba is receiving the protection and recognition it deserves. The Apache have received an Arizona Heritage Fund grant to help preserve the architectural integrity of the ruins and develop a new visitor-use plan for the site.

43 CASA MALPAIS ARCHAEOLOGICAL PARK

318 E. Main St.
Springerville, AZ 85938
(928) 333-5375

NEAREST SUPPLY CENTER:
Springerville, Arizona

HIGHLIGHTS: The ruins of
the Mogollon village at Casa
Malpais overlook a broad,
fertile valley, and the site
offers spectacular views of
some of Arizona's tallest
mountain peaks.

INTERPRETATION: The visitor
center/museum provides
guided tours—the only way
to access the ruins.

SEASONS OPEN: All seasons

HOURS OF OPERATION: Tours
depart at 9 a.m., 11 a.m.,
and 2 p.m. daily.

FEE AREA: Yes

ACCESS ROAD: Paved

DIRECTIONS: Springerville
is on US 60, about 25 miles
west of the New Mexico
border. Look for signs
directing visitors to the
Casa Malpais site.

The Little Colorado River flows from its source high up in the majestic White Mountains to the valley below. As the water cuts across the barren land, it takes an easterly course past the remains of numerous prehistoric villages and rock-art sites in the fertile floodplain around Nutrioso Creek. But the village at Casa Malpais stands out from the others in the area. Deeply trenched canyons carpeted by thick deposits of eroded soil weave their way through the layers of volcanic rock surrounding the site. The Mogollon ruins are nestled in one of these trenches at the base of an 80-foot ledge, and petroglyphs etched on the sheer rock walls mark the ancient people's presence here.

The prehistoric Mogollons are believed to have arrived in the rugged area as early as A.D. 700, when their nomadic life focused on hunting and gathering. Experts believe that Mesoamerican cultures first introduced the techniques of raising corn, squash, and other crops to the Mogollons, who came to depend more and more on domestic crops for food. By A.D. 1000, farming was their primary way of life, and the fertile and well-watered soil around Nutrioso Creek was perfect for their agricultural endeavors.

The Mogollons also progressed from their pithouse dwellings to a Pueblo community. The "new" buildings at Casa Malpais, constructed using basalt found in the area, were probably completed by A.D. 1250. Large rocks were held in place by thick layers of mud mortar and chinked with smaller stones to ensure tightness. The builders also incorporated deep natural fissures in the lava into the pueblo's construction, and in some cases the exterior walls of this 50-room pueblo encased the natural cave formations left behind by volcanic flows.

The imposing size of the pueblo and the presence of the Great Kiva at Casa Malpais cause some archaeologists to believe that the site was used for regional gatherings and ceremonies, bringing together people from numerous villages along the far-reaching river. Another ruin at Casa Malpais also causes speculation among experts. The footprint of the structure is all that remains, but the original building is believed to have served as an astrological observatory. This irregular oval structure has five small openings that may have enabled the ancient Mogollons to observe the sun's alignment during solstice and equinox.

The burial sites at Casa Malpais are also intriguing and unique. Hundreds of people were thought to have been buried in the chambers here, though the significance of the deep network of graves is unknown. The burial sites are closed to the public due to safety concerns.

UTE MOUNTAIN UTE RESERVATION

Shiprock
Farmington
574
Aztec
59
Aztec Ruins National Monument
Navajo City
64
Chama
17
Blanco
GOBERNADOR CANYON
58
Bloomfield
57
Gobernador
LARGO CANYON
550
84
Taos
371
Blanco Trading Post
57
Nageezi
7900
Chetro Ketl
Kin Kletso
Pueblo del Arroyo
Una Vida
Casa Rinconada
7950
56
Chaco Culture National Historical Park
Cuba
491
NAVAJO RESERVATION
57
14
9
Crownpoint
Borrego Pass
48
Gallup
602
HIST. **66**
47
19
Prewitt
509
ZUNI RESERVATION
53
El Morro
46
605
Grants
44
Zuni
36
48 TH
TH
El Malpais National Monument
117

Los Alamos
502
Tsankawi
Pojoaque
4
White Rock
54
Bandelier National Monument
Painted Cave
55
Jemez Springs
SANTA FE
285
Pecos National Historical Park
63
53
Las Veg
exit 299
exit 307
550
52
Bernalillo
exit 242
Petroglyph National Monument
51
ALBUQUERQUE
exit 154
Moriarty
40
25
41
55
60
Quarai Ruins
Mountainair
50
Willard
Vaughn
Abo Ruins
Bernardo
60
54
Gran Quivira Ruins
55
San Antonio
380
25
Carrizozo
Rio Grande
Three Rivers
49
Three Rivers
45
Gila Cliff Dwellings National Monument
15
ALAMOGORDO
180
35
152
25
Silver City
152
180
70
25
180
LAS CRUCES
Lordsburg
Deming
10
10
EL PASO

SANGRE DE CRISTO MOUNTAINS
Rio Grande

Gila Cliff Dwellings National Monument;
Above: Three Rivers Petroglyph Site

New Mexico

*Pecos National Historical Park;
Far left: Salinas Pueblo
Missions National Monument*

44 ZUNI PUEBLO

Pueblo of Zuni Tourism
Department
P.O. Box 339
Zuni, NM 87327
(505) 782-7238

NEAREST SUPPLY CENTER:
Zuni, New Mexico

HIGHLIGHTS: The sites at
Zuni Pueblo, on the present-
day Zuni Reservation, speak
to the success and ingenuity
of the Zuni culture, which
thrived here in the 13th
century.

INTERPRETATION: Visitor
center, museum, and guided
tours. Tours and/or prior
permission are required
to visit the sites. Call for
information.

SEASONS OPEN: All seasons

HOURS OF OPERATION:
All hours

FEE AREA: No

ACCESS ROAD: Dirt, which is
impassable after heavy rains

DIRECTIONS: Zuni Pueblo is
35 miles southwest of Gallup.
From I-40 in Gallup, take
NM 602 south to NM 53,
and head west to reach
the pueblo.

NOTE: The people of Zuni
Pueblo request that all visitors
stop at the visitor center in
the heart of town before
starting their exploration. A
permit is required in order
to photograph antiquities,
structures, or people at Zuni
Pueblo. Several of the sites
at Zuni Pueblo can only be
accessed on a guided tour.

*"When I was a little girl, my grandmother used to
tell us kids stories about the old ancestors and how,
at one time, we Zuni people lived on the bluffs on
top of El Morro. . ."*

These are the words of a native Zuni woman
who's lived most of her life in the ancestral
homeland of her people. She's also a tour guide
for the museum at Zuni Pueblo, and when she
speaks about the ruins at Hawikuh, she does so
with both passion and authority.

There are two ruin sites that have been
authorized by the Zuni people for public view.
Both sites are well interpreted by native guides.

The tour to **Village of the Great Kiva** is the
longer of the two. This partially excavated site,
named for its two ceremonial kivas, offers an
equal mixture of vivid history and cultural rich-
ness. Guides provide detailed information about
the ancestral use of the kivas and the important
spiritual role these structures played in the
development and conservation of the ancient
Zuni traditions and culture. This site also has a
number of rock-art panels painted by ancestral
Zuni artisans.

The pueblo structures are believed to have
been heavily influenced by the Chacoan culture
from which the Zuni people claim to have
descended. At the time of its peak, the village
may have included as many as 18 rooms together
with the two large kivas.

A tour to **Hawikuh,** the second site, will
definitely inspire the history buff. Only small
sections of walls are exposed; however, the rich
cultural history of the site is well worth the
time it takes to explore these ruins. Legend has it that eight survivors of a
Spanish shipwreck roamed the deserts and plains of Texas and New Mexico for
more than eight years before arriving in the Zuni homeland. Among the survivors
were Cabeza de Vaca and his Moorish slave Esteban. After spending time with the
peaceful Zuni and experiencing their friendship and generosity, the foreigners

returned to Mexico City filled with fantastic stories about the people they had encountered and the bustling cities in the midst of desert lands. These accounts seemed to match the old Spanish legend of The Seven Cities of Cibola and inspired the adventurous Spaniards to set off on an exploration.

Sponsored by the Spanish monarchy, Esteban returned to the Zuni homeland in 1539, this time in the company of Fray Marcos de Niza, who was installed as the group leader. Esteban went ahead to scout the land for riches, and word came back to Fray Marcos that he had arrived at the Zuni village of Hawikuh. It was in May, the season of Zuni ceremonies honoring the annual arrival of the sacred kachinas back from their winter place. However, instead of kachinas, the Zuni saw the dark-skinned figure of Esteban, regaled in colorful feathers and approaching their village. At first, the people thought him a heavenly figure, but that proved to be far from the case.

Esteban made outrageous demands for turquoise and the favor of Zuni women, and he threatened reprisal from a powerful force camped not far from Hawikuh. The Zuni chiefs were insulted by the demands made by the Moor. They took Esteban prisoner and, after short deliberation, put him to death for his guile.

Nonetheless, Fray Marcos returned to Mexico City with more stories of riches and wonder beyond belief. In 1540, Francisco Vasquez de Coronado marched north toward Hawikuh with more than 300 soldiers and 1,000 native people, a force never before witnessed in the deserts of the Southwest. Coronado overran peaceful Hawikuh, and, from his new outpost within the Zuni homeland, he led his army with vengeance and vigor through many other pueblo villages. So began the Spanish occupation of present-day New Mexico, darkened by bloodshed, slavery, and the eventual demise of the Pueblo people. The pueblo at Hawikuh was abandoned soon after the Pueblo Rebellion in 1680, and it was never reoccupied.

The ruins at Hawikuh and other sites in the Zuni homeland were excavated between 1917 and 1923. The 400-room pueblo was studied and backfilled to ensure its protection. The ruins of a 17th-century mission built during the Spanish occupation were also studied. This mission, named La Purisima Concepcion de Hawikuh, was one of many destroyed during the Pueblo Revolt. The archaeological sites at Zuni Pueblo are sacred to the people whose ancestors called this place home and should not be entered without a Zuni guide.

Hawikuh ruins

45 GILA CLIFF DWELLINGS NATIONAL MONUMENT

HC 68 Box 100
Silver City, NM 88061
(505) 536-9461

NEAREST SUPPLY CENTER:
Silver City, New Mexico

HIGHLIGHTS: The beautifully preserved ruins at Gila Cliff Dwellings National Monument display the architecture and ingenuity of the Mogollon people, who inhabited this region long ago.

LEVEL OF INTERPRETATION:
Visitor center, guided and self-guided tours, and interpretive panels

SEASONS OPEN: All seasons

HOURS OF OPERATION:
Summer, 8 a.m. to 6 p.m. (the visitor center closes at 5 p.m.); winter, 9 a.m. to 4 p.m. (the visitor center is open from 8 a.m. to 4:30 p.m.)

FEE AREA: Yes

ACCESS ROAD: Paved

DIRECTIONS: Gila Cliff Dwellings National Monument sits at the end of NM 15, 44 miles north of the historic town of Silver City. Due to the winding nature of this road, the drive takes roughly 90 minutes. (The park service recommends that vehicles more than 20 feet in length take NM 35, east of Silver City, to reach the site.)

Gila Cliff Dwellings

The ancient Mogollon culture is believed to have evolved from Archaic hunters and gatherers who roamed throughout the Southwest thousands of years ago. Their close ties to the Mesoamerican people living south of present-day New Mexico probably exposed the ancient Mogollons to agriculture at a very early stage of their cultural advancement. Some experts believe it was the Mogollon people who, in turn, introduced corn to the Ancestral Puebloan (Anasazi) cultures.

Traces of prehistoric Mogollon people have been discovered throughout the region now known as Gila National Forest. Archaeologists believe the first people to settle here were probably attracted by the plentiful supply of water, rich soil, and abundant plants and wildlife found in the region. A few isolated sites dating back as far as A.D. 200 serve as the earliest substantial archaeological record of the Mogollon culture here. However, it is from the period between A.D. 200 and 1400 that experts have learned most of what they know today about these creative and enduring people.

Mogollon architecture, like that of most ancient civilizations throughout the Southwest, evolved from pithouse to pueblo around A.D. 1200. Significant cultural advancements began to take place simultaneously, as can be seen by the refined and unique pottery style the people adapted during their time in the Gila

region. Other artifacts uncovered in the area suggest the Mogollons also traded goods with the Hohokam as well as the Anasazi, who influenced the people at Gila both culturally and socially.

The cliff dwellings here, which were likely constructed between A.D. 1270 and 1280, are strikingly Anasazi in appearance. The builders at Gila Cliff Dwellings enclosed existing caves with block-and-mortar facing that runs from the floor of the alcove to the natural roof above. Stone walls inside the structure divided the space into individual rooms. A thick coating of black soot from the fires used for cooking and to warm the dwellings still covers the overhanging roof.

Below the cliff dwellings, farmers grew crops while others hunted wild game in the thickly timbered slopes. Bone fragments uncovered during excavations show that

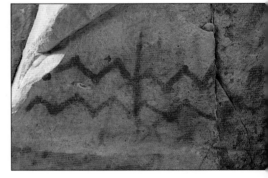

two of the most common species of wild game hunted by the prehistoric Mogollons were rabbits and mule deer. Despite the plentiful resources here, the Gila Cliff Dwellings, like so many sites in the Southwest, were suddenly abandoned without apparent reason. The people were gone by A.D. 1300, less than four decades after their arrival.

The Gila Cliff Dwellings are now managed and protected by the National Park Service, which maintains an informative visitor center in the area. The center should be your first stop if you plan to visit the cliff dwellings. Be sure to get a map of the area and ask for specific directions. The hike to the dwelling site is relaxing and crosses some beautiful and rugged canyon country.

46 EL MORRO NATIONAL MONUMENT

HC 61 Box 43
Ramah, NM 87321-9603
(505) 783-4226

NEAREST SUPPLY CENTER:
Zuni or Grants, New Mexico

HIGHLIGHTS: Prehistoric
petroglyphs mix with a
large collection of Spanish
signatures and writings at
Inscription Rock in El Morro
National Monument, telling
the saga of human presence
here.

INTERPRETATION: Visitor center,
exhibits, and self-guided
tours

SEASONS OPEN: All seasons

HOURS OF OPERATION: Visitor
center, 9 a.m. to 5 p.m.; trails,
9 a.m. to 4 p.m.

FEE AREA: Yes

ACCESS ROAD: Paved

DIRECTIONS: El Morro National
Monument is 43 miles southwest of Grants, which is west
of Albuquerque on I-40. Turn
left on NM 53 at Grants; the
intersection is clearly marked
with signs for El Morro and
El Malpais National Monu-
ments and the town of Zuni.

Atsinna Pueblo ruins

Early people first built small pithouse encampments in the area around what is now Atsinna Pueblo in A.D. 700. These settlements began to grow in size as the society continued to develop, eventually becoming less reliant on hunting and gathering and more dependent on domestic crops. With this shift, the ancient people began building more permanent residential structures and storage facilities above ground, like those atop the El Morro bluff. The structure that remains at the site today consists of about 12 masonry rooms and a large kiva, which have been excavated, stabilized, and left exposed for public view. Scholars believe the pueblo at Atsinna could have stretched as far as 300 feet across the mesa at one time.

The Zuni inhabitants, like most other Ancestral Puebloan (Anasazi) people of the period, relied on irrigated crops to sustain them. Fields were tended in the valleys below the mesa and the harvested crops were hauled in baskets to the mesa-top to be processed and stored within the pueblo. Food and water were probably

carried to the pueblo in large baskets or pottery vessels made by the artisans of the village. This pottery features a style unique to the Zuni people, partly due to their isolation from other tribes.

The builders of the Atsinna Pueblo took advantage of an abundance of raw materials found around the mesa at El Morro. Sandstone slabs were chiseled from natural formations and fashioned into square building blocks. These blocks were held in place by thick layers of mortar blended from clay soils, with small pebbles and wedge-shaped stones inserted between the rows to reinforce them.

Some experts believe the prehistoric people who lived in the El Morro pueblos may have suffered stress from outside invaders, causing the inhabitants to construct their dwellings far from the fields they tended and the main source of their drinking water—a deep, clear pool filled, for the most part, by seasonal runoff from the mesa above. Close examination of the sandstone face around the pool will reveal the ancient handholds and footholds used by the Zuni as they carried water to the mesatops.

The pool was a frequent stopping place for travelers in the Rio Grande Valley as well, and the messages, signatures, and symbols they left behind on Inscription Rock span prehistoric and historic times, bringing significance to the name Atsinna which, in the Zuni language, means "writing on the rock." Early inhabitants etched images on sandstone, and the Spanish conquistadors who came to the region in search of riches left their mark on the rock here, too. A trip to the monument, and particularly to Inscription Rock, provides visitors with a sense of the passage of time and the diversity of people who frequented this place—some striving for survival within a harsh landscape and others driven by an insatiable hunger for gold.

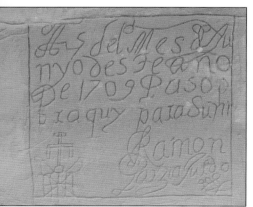

Carvings and etchings at Inscription Rock

El Morro

47 CASAMERO PUEBLO

Bureau of Land Management
Rio Puerco Resource Area
435 Montano NE
Albuquerque, NM 87107-4935
(505) 761-8704

NEAREST SUPPLY CENTER:
Grants, New Mexico

HIGHLIGHTS: The pueblo village at Casamero is well-preserved and is a perfect example of a Chacoan outlier community.

INTERPRETATION:
Interpretive panels

SEASONS OPEN: All seasons

HOURS OF OPERATION:
All hours

FEE AREA: No

ACCESS ROAD: Paved

DIRECTIONS: Casamero Pueblo is 19 miles west of Grants. At the Prewitt exit on I-40, proceed to Historic Route 66, turn right, and travel east for about 1 mile to County Road 19. (This intersection is well marked.) Turn left on CR 19, drive 4 miles north, and look for a small pullout on the left side of the road shortly after crossing the railroad tracks. A short hiking trail leads to the pueblo site.

Huge sandstone cliffs rise beautifully behind the ancient pueblo ruins at Casamero. The landscape is brilliantly painted in the desert light and looks much as it must have when Ancestral Puebloan people lived here centuries ago.

The village at Casamero Pueblo, believed to have been built and occupied between A.D. 1000 and 1125, is a classic example of an outlier community associated with the thriving Chacoan culture. The walls that remain standing at the site feature a beautiful pattern of gray rock slabs bound between generous layers of red clay—architectural traits associated with the ancient builders of Chaco Canyon. The physical layout of the village mirrors Chacoan communities as well. Archaeologists who have studied the site think the original pueblo at Casamero contained 22 rooms on the ground floor, six second-story rooms on the west side, and an enclosed kiva in the northeast section of the pueblo.

A second ceremonial kiva remains buried about 200 feet southwest of the exposed pueblo site. To the east, across the draw, there is an unexcavated pueblo structure as well as the remains of a prehistoric road that is believed to have connected the two pueblos. Additional roads have also been discovered in the area and lead across the desert to the west. These roads, as well as the substantial volume of trade goods found throughout the area, have helped archaeologists and anthropologists link places like Casamero Pueblo to the vast cultural network and thriving trade economy that existed for generations within Chaco Canyon. Could Casamero Pueblo have been a remote trading post or an important ceremonial site along the ancient Chacoan Road? As research continues, the answers to these and many other questions surrounding outlying communities like Casamero Pueblo may be found.

Casamero Pueblo has endured considerable vandalism throughout its recent past. Fortunately, the Bureau of Land Management completely stabilized the pueblo in 1976 and erected a number of interpretive signs to help visitors learn of the rich cultural history at the area. The BLM continues to manage the site as an educational area for the public.

48 ZUNI–ACOMA TRAIL

123 E. Roosevelt Ave.
Grants, NM 87020
(505) 783-4774

NEAREST SUPPLY CENTER:
Zuni, New Mexico

HIGHLIGHTS: This trail, part of an extensive system of trails that spread across the desert for hundreds of miles, once connected the pueblos at Zuni and Acoma.

INTERPRETATION:
Interpretive panels

SEASONS OPEN: All seasons

HOURS OF OPERATION:
All hours

FEE AREA: No

ACCESS ROAD: Paved

DIRECTIONS: The Zuni–Acoma Trail traverses El Malpais National Monument. The east end of the trail begins at NM 117, 16 miles south of its intersection with I-40. The pullout and parking lot at the east trailhead are clearly marked. The west trailhead is on NM 53, 15 miles south of its inter-section with I-40. There are small visitor centers at both ends of the trail.

NOTE: This trail is very challenging and should only be attempted in its entirety with prior planning and a vehicle shuttle. The route, marked by rock cairns, is often faint, and the rock can be jagged and sharp in places. Be sure to bring plenty of water and sun protection.

The Zuni–Acoma Trail was the primary travel route that linked the growing pueblo villages of Acoma and Zuni. The trail crosses a broad, sweeping valley that was formed about 260 million years ago as sandy deposits on the ancient seafloor hardened after the sea retreated, forming what is known today as the Colorado Plateau. The sandstone base eroded over time and was eventually covered by a series of lava flows that filled the valley. Ancestral Zuni and Acoma traditions speak about the "fiery times" during which the lava was forced to the surface where it hardened into jagged rock.

The seven-mile portion of the Zuni–Acoma Trail that can be traveled by hikers today should be approached with caution. Even though the ancient people are thought to have crossed the sharp lava flows in sandals fashioned only with woven yucca fibers, thick-soled hiking boots are strongly recommended in order to avoid bruised or cut feet.

The ancient trail is marked by a series of rock cairns, which, on occasion, can be difficult to locate. Hikers should strive to stay on the trail, as it is hard to regain the path once you stray from it. Due to the extreme heat generated by the black rocks, carry plenty of water and try to get an early start. It is very important to give yourself an ample amount of time to cross the seven miles of rugged terrain.

Like any place within the culturally rich regions of the Southwest, the chance of coming across ancient artifacts is always present. Please remember that this is not only an ancient trail protected by federal antiquity laws, but it is also an important part of the sacred landscape of both the Zuni and Acoma people. The trail and its surrounding area must be treated with respect. Artifacts should be left in place for others to enjoy.

49 THREE RIVERS PETROGLYPH SITE

Bureau of Land Management
Caballo Resource Area
1800 Marquess
Las Cruces, NM 88005
(505) 525-8228

NEAREST SUPPLY CENTER:
Three Rivers, New Mexico

HIGHLIGHTS: The Three Rivers Petroglyph Site contains more than 20,000 individual images, making it one of the most extensive collections of rock art in the Southwest.

INTERPRETATION:
Interpretive panels

SEASONS OPEN: All seasons

HOURS OF OPERATION:
All hours

FEE AREA: Yes

ACCESS ROAD: Paved

DIRECTIONS: Three Rivers Petroglyph Site is located 30 miles north of Alamogordo on US 54 in the center of southern New Mexico. At the small town of Three Rivers, turn east and proceed 5 miles to the site parking lot.

The eye of an artist is said to be connected more closely to the spiritual soul than to the human brain. Surely this must have been the case for the ancient artists who carved their petroglyphs onto the dark rocks at what is now the Three Rivers Petroglyph Site. The images themselves follow the gradual progression of the Mogollon people as their dwellings grew from crude pithouses into pueblo-style villages and their artistic style and craftsmanship became more refined.

The petroglyphs at Three Rivers are primarily the work of the Jornada Mogollon, a people who once lived and farmed in the area around the isolated site. Each of the more than 20,000 images tells a story; some display day-to-day life during prehistoric times, while others show people hunting wild animals in the distant mountains or depict the deep ceremonial customs and traditions of the ancient Mogollons. Some archaeologists believe that important changes within Mogollon society were recorded on these petroglyph panels, which span the Mogollon occupation here, from A.D. 900 to 1400.

The Three Rivers site covers approximately 50 acres with spectacular views of the Tularosa Basin and the surrounding rugged mountains bordering the area. There are two trails that depart from the visitor center parking lot. One proceeds up a small hill to petroglyph panels and the other leads to a small ruin site south of the petroglyphs. Neither hike is very demanding; however, the small elevation gain feels greater on a hot, sunny day!

50 SALINAS PUEBLO MISSIONS NATIONAL MONUMENT

P.O. Box 517
Mountainair, NM 87036
(505) 847-2585

NEAREST SUPPLY CENTER:
Mountainair, New Mexico

HIGHLIGHTS: The buildings
at the monument are relics
of both the thriving Pueblo
culture and the Spanish conquest and missionary effort.

INTERPRETATION: Museum,
interpretive panels, and
self-guided tours

HOURS OF OPERATION:
Summer, 9 a.m. to 6 p.m.;
winter, 9 a.m. to 5 p.m.

SEASONS OPEN: All seasons

FEE AREA: Yes

ACCESS ROAD: Paved

DIRECTIONS: The monument
headquarters are at the
intersection of US 60 and
NM 55, just outside the
town of Mountainair.

A round A.D. 600, pithouse villages began to spring up across the Estancia Basin. The subterranean dwellings were of crude construction, as mud huts with thatched roofs served as suitable shelters for these nomadic people. However, as trade and contact between the various cultures started to develop, and agriculture became the focus of their society, the architecture in the Estancia Basin began to change. The people started to build more permanent structures around A.D. 900, which seems to have been influenced by both the Mogollon civilization to the south, and the Ancestral Puebloan (Anasazi) culture of Chaco Canyon some 200 miles to the north.

In A.D. 1300, a drought forced the residents of Anasazi villages like those in Mesa Verde, in Colorado, to migrate south, in the direction of much-needed water. Many of these displaced farmers arrived in the Estancia Basin, and they brought the benefits of their culture with them. Three pueblos were significantly developed during and after this migration, and each grew to house hundreds of people.

Abo was built at the base of the Manzano Mountains below Abo Pass. Several natural springs near the site provided water for the fields. The stone village here

Opposite and above: Quarai Ruins

was also situated along a primary trade route through the mountain pass, which led to the Rio Grande valley, and this location served as an economic stimulus for the growing community.

Quarai sits in the forest below the Manzano Mountains and is also within reach of several springs. The wooded area around the village gave people the timber used for building and cooking. Archaeological studies have determined that people here probably cooked outdoors. However, the relatively high altitude of the basin and the subsequent harsh winters would have forced residents to stay within the shelter of their pueblos during the cold months.

Las Humanas sits alongside Chupadero Mesa, on the southern edge of the Estancia Basin. The pueblo, built from the gray stones found in the area, once contained more than 240 rooms. The living

Photos above: Quarai Ruins

Abo Ruins

Gran Quivira Ruins

quarters were built around a large kiva—a sign of the importance of ceremony in the ancient people's lives.

The farmers who lived at Las Humanas may have had a more difficult life than their counterparts at Abo and Quarai, because the area around the pueblo was not endowed with much water. These people used great ingenuity, constructing catchments, dams, canals, and wells to conserve and distribute precious water.

What it lacked in water resources, however, Las Humanas made up for in trade. The pueblo's proximity to the wandering tribes of the plains made it a good stop on the trade network, and artifacts discovered at the site display a wide range of goods that came to Las Humanas from people and places hundreds of miles away.

Gran Quivira Ruins

Interestingly, the residents of Abo, Quarai, and Las Humanas retained their dependence on hunting and gathering throughout their occupation here, unlike most native people of the Rio Grande Valley. Archaeological studies have uncovered a great number of animal bones in the middens, or trash heaps, near the sites, suggesting that the people here relied on hunting despite the development of their agriculture.

In 1598, the Spanish arrived in the basin and the peaceful and prosperous culture that had been living there for centuries was suddenly and irreparably changed. The native people were forced to sign the "Act of Obedience" making them subjects of the Spanish crown, and, under the system of *encomienda* were required to pay tribute in either goods, such as crops, or services, such as slave labor.

The Franciscan Order of the Holy Catholic Church arrived as well, with the aim of extending the church's influence in the new world and saving the souls of the "savages" they met along the way. Huge missions, built by the native people, were erected near the pueblos in what the Spanish called the Salinas District, due to the salt flats there. The Indians' way of life was drastically altered, and their own sense of spirituality was overshadowed by the religious beliefs of their Spanish rulers.

But it was the hand of nature that would finally destroy the people of Estancia Basin. Drought struck in the early 1660s, and hundreds of Indians, who had left their farming to build the imposing missions, were left with little food in their storage rooms and a string of bad harvests. In 1668 alone, 450 native people in Las Humanas died from hunger. Disease followed on the heels of the drought, killing native people and Spanish settlers alike, and the springs at both Abo and Quarai dried to a trickle around 1677, sealing the fate of the great pueblos. Those who survived are thought to have migrated north into the Galisteo Basin, never to return to their once-loved land at Estancia.

51 PETROGLYPH NATIONAL MONUMENT

6001 Unser Blvd. NW
Albuquerque, NM 87120
(505) 899-0205

NEAREST SUPPLY CENTER:
Albuquerque, New Mexico

HIGHLIGHTS: This spectacular
rock-art site includes images
that span thousands of years
—from the Archaic period to
the 1800s.

INTERPRETATION: Visitor center
and self-guided tours

SEASONS OPEN: All seasons

HOURS OPEN: All hours (call
for hours at the various visitor
centers)

ACCESS ROAD: Paved

DIRECTIONS: Petroglyph
National Monument is west
of Albuquerque. Head west
on I-40 from its intersection
with I-25 for approximately
6 miles to Exit 154, and
proceed north on Unser
Boulevard for 3 miles to the
visitor center. The route is
clearly marked and easy to
follow.

The story of Petroglyph National Monument actually begins more than 110,000 years ago as molten lava surged through a crack in the earth's surface and covered the surrounding landscape. Over time, the forces of erosion went to work, carving and sculpting the jagged edges of the escarpment we know today as West Mesa.

Millions of years later, Archaic nomads began to roam across the desert as they followed herds of migrating animals. Scholars believe it was in these early years of life on the harsh landscape that ancient people first began to peck their petroglyphs onto the volcanic stones scattered across West Mesa. These first markings, laid in place by early nomads, were followed by the art of Ancestral Puebloans (Anasazi). It is unclear whether these early Puebloan people resided in villages in the immediate vicinity of West Mesa or simply left their art behind as they passed through the rugged area in search of a more suitable homeland.

The patina, or desert varnish, that had darkened the surface of the boulders made a perfect canvas for these prehistoric artists to peck images into the rock, exposing the lighter color underneath. Over time, more than 15,000 petroglyphs were chiseled on the rocks here, and the oldest are believed to have been designed more than 2,500 years ago. The most common petroglyphs at the monument have been termed the Rio Grande Style and date back to roughly A.D. 1300.

The primal pictures display anthropomorphic and zoomorphic figures, while later images depict ritual ceremonies, animal totems inspiring good fortune, and scenes relating to everyday life. Images of macaws, which were brought to the Southwest from the depths of Mexico, tell of trade with other cultures, while bears and badgers represent the spiritual connection the ancestors felt with the wild creatures. Scenes reflecting the arrival of the Spanish are also included in the broad mix of images. These events are chronicled by the appearance of Christian crosses, which are believed to have been left either by converted indigenous people or Spanish shepherds in the 1700s or 1800s.

A number of well-maintained trails lead to various petroglyph sites in the monument. It is a good idea to begin with a stop at the visitor center, where rangers can help you select a route that will best suit your time and interest. Petroglyph National Monument is crowded during peak times of the year due to its proximity to Albuquerque. However, you can enjoy a sense of solitude here in the early morning hours.

52 CORONADO STATE MONUMENT

485 Kuaua Rd.
Bernalillo, NM 87004
(505) 867-5351

NEAREST SUPPLY CENTER:
Bernalillo, New Mexico

HIGHLIGHTS: This scenic park and its museum hold the historic remnants of the Kuaua Anasazi as well as the Spanish conquistadors who explored the land during the 16th century.

INTERPRETATION: Visitors center, museum, interpretive panels, and self-guided tours

SEASONS OPEN: All seasons

HOURS OF OPERATION:
8:30 a.m. to 4:30 p.m.;
closed Tuesday

FEE AREA: Yes

ACCESS ROAD: Paved

DIRECTIONS: Coronado State Monument is just off US 550 (formerly NM 44), 1 mile west of Bernalillo, which is approximately 15 miles north of Albuquerque on I-25, at Exit 242.

The lush banks and sweeping floodplains of the Rio Grande attracted prehistoric people migrating through the Southwest in search of reliable water for their agriculture. Thousands of Ancestral Puebloan (Anasazi) people built villages up and down the Rio Grande Valley and planted crops in the fertile floodplain. The vegetation that thrived along the Rio Grande supplemented the farming efforts and also provided cover and refuge for small animals, birds, and reptiles, which the Anasazi hunted along with big game like deer and elk.

Kuaua Pueblo is one of the many sites that blossomed along the Rio Grande. Construction on the first 40-room structure of this pueblo began around A.D. 1300, and, in the years that followed, as many as 1,200 rooms were added to the village. Many of the room blocks were multi-storied and surrounded the three central plazas that held a number of ceremonial kivas.

Two of the kivas uncovered at Kuaua are round. The third kiva, which today bears the name Kiva III, is rectangular and has been excavated and fully restored. Over the many years

Kiva interior, Kuaua Ruins

of occupation of Kuaua Pueblo, ancient craftsmen applied as many as 87 layers of adobe plaster to the interior walls of Kiva III. Many of these layers were adorned with beautifully painted murals, and the restoration efforts performed at the Kuaua Pueblo site have focused on recovering and restoring these artistic treasures. Some of the original murals are on display in the small museum at Coronado State Monument, and reproductions have been painted on the walls of Kiva III. They depict scenes of a mystic quality, including human figures, animals, birds, snakes, and fish.

During the winter of 1540–1541, the army of Francisco Vasquez de Coronado, for whom the monument has since been named, occupied a pueblo village near Kuaua. His forces must have appeared colossal to the indigenous people, for the army included a total of 300 soldiers, 1,000 natives, and more than 1,500 horses and mules. During the long winter months, Coronado's soldiers may have confiscated food and other supplies from the native people, pillaged the surrounding pueblos, and even molested the native women.

When spring finally arrived, Coronado's army departed to continue their unsuccessful search for the famed Seven Cities of Cibola. The destruction and fear they left behind was long remembered by the Puebloan people in the region and marked the beginning of an era of conflict between the Europeans and the native people of the Southwest.

Kuaua Ruins

53 PECOS NATIONAL HISTORICAL PARK

P.O. Box 418
Pecos, NM 87552-0418
(505) 757-6414

NEAREST SUPPLY CENTER:
Pecos, New Mexico

HIGHLIGHTS: This impressive park spans more than 12,000 years of human history. Native people, Spanish colonizers, traders on the Santa Fe Trail, Civil War soldiers, and ranchers have all left footprints on the landscape here.

INTERPRETATION: Visitor center, exhibits, and ranger-guided and self-guided tours

SEASONS OPEN: All seasons

HOURS OF OPERATION:
Summer, 8 a.m. to 6 p.m.; winter, 8 a.m. to 4:30 p.m.

FEE AREA: Yes

ACCESS ROAD: Paved

DIRECTIONS: Pecos National Historical Park is approximately 25 miles east of Santa Fe, off of I-25. Take either Exit 299 or Exit 307 onto NM 63 and proceed to the park.

The flowing water of the Pecos River and the abundant plants and animals in the area undoubtedly attracted the first people who made permanent settlements in this beautiful territory bordered by the Sangre de Cristo Mountains. They arrived in the area sometime around A.D. 800, probably migrating from the Rio Grande Valley. As the people here began farming the rich land, their lives became more sedentary, and crude pithouses were replaced by block-and-mortar pueblos. By A.D. 1250, these pueblo villages had grown larger as the ancient farmers banded together in tighter, more efficient communities.

By A.D. 1450, the Pecos Pueblo had reached a height of five stories and housed as many as 2,000 inhabitants. Its location, with the large farming communities of the Rio Grande Valley to the west and the Great Plains settlements to the east, made Pecos Pueblo a central stop on the busy trade network. Textiles, pottery, turquoise, crops, dried bison meat, and bison robes were some of the more precious items traded among the people of the Southwest during this prosperous time.

In A.D. 1540, the first sound of musket fire announced the presence of Francisco Vasquez de Coronado in the Zuni village of Hawikuh. It wasn't long before the invading army, mounted upon the first horses the native people had ever seen, arrived in the Pecos River Valley. The Pueblo people welcomed the foreigners and marveled at their colorful dress and the beauty of the strange animals on which they rode. After staying with the people of Pecos for a short time, and

Opposite and above: Pecos Pueblo and Mission Ruins

Our Lady of the Angels of Porciuncula Mission

apparently without strife, the army pressed on in search of a land reported to harbor wealth beyond Coronado's wildest dreams.

Six decades later, however, the Spanish returned to Pecos Pueblo, this time to stay. They planned to colonize the area, declaring themselves to be the new masters of the rich agricultural region, and set about to convert the indigenous people into loyal, Christian subjects of the Crown. Under the ruling hand of Franciscan priests, the native people's traditional ceremonies and spiritual customs were forbidden, and they also were forced to build a huge mission just east of their pueblos.

A thick roof of dark clouds hung over the southern end of the Sangre de Cristo Mountains the afternoon we drove toward the ancient pueblo ruins and old Spanish mission at Pecos National Historical Park. A gentle breeze slowly moved the overhanging clouds as the hues of gray and black intermingled.

It was late November, and we'd decided to camp for the night in the Santa Fe National Forest, just north of the monument. We awakened the next morning to eight inches of fresh snow, which spread like a blanket across the ruins. What a fitting welcome for a set of northern visitors like Cathie and me! We walked through the ankle-deep snow, plowing our own path as we moved our cameras from site to site. As the morning began to warm, we watched the melting snow drip off the ruins and roll like tears down the brown adobe walls of the historic Mission of Our Lady of the Angels of Porciuncula.

Pecos is a place of contrasts as stark as red earth against white snow. The footprint of the prehistoric pueblo stands beside the decaying Spanish mission— both were built by the same hands, but driven by different motives and desires. This place saw freedom and servitude, Catholicism and kivas, a farming culture and one bent on conquest.

We watched the dry, parched soil drink up the freshly melted snow, until all that remained of the water was an outline—a footprint —like much of what is left at Pecos. Soon our snowy morning would be nothing but a memory.

Pecos Pueblo and Mission Ruins

While the Franciscans were Christianizing the native people, Spanish officials collected food and other commodities from the natives as "tributes" to the Spanish Crown. All across the Southwest, the heavy hand of Spanish rule was crushing the indigenous people, and in 1680 the Indians revolted en masse. Perhaps because it was so unexpected, the Pueblo Rebellion was a success. The Spanish were driven back across the Mexican border and the missions were virtually destroyed by angry natives. Twelve years later, however, the Spanish returned to reclaim their empire and forced the Pueblo people to build another mission at Pecos.

Kiva interior

Life for the Puebloan people of Pecos continued to fall apart over the next century, and by 1839 their once-burgeoning population had only 17 members left. Disease, continuing raids by enemy tribes, and a long-lasting drought shook the very roots of the pueblo community. The remaining inhabitants of Pecos took refuge in Jemez Pueblo, west of Pecos, and their descendents remain there to this day.

Several other sites of interest here are the Forked Lightning Ranch, a stretch of the Santa Fe Trail, and the site of the Civil War battle of Glorieta Pass. Ranger-guided tours are required to access these historic sites.

Pecos Pueblo and Mission Ruins

54 BANDELIER NATIONAL MONUMENT

15 Entrance Rd.
Los Alamos, NM 87544
(505) 672-3861

NEAREST SUPPLY CENTER:
White Rock, New Mexico

HIGHLIGHTS: The Archaic sites and Ancestral Puebloan dwellings at Bandelier National Monument, accented by the breathtaking backdrop of mesas and sheer, sandstone cliffs, span thousands of years of human occupation.

INTERPRETATION: Visitor center, interpretive panels, and self-guided tours

SEASONS OPEN: All seasons

HOURS OF OPERATION: All hours (call for seasonal hours at the visitor center)

FEE AREA: Yes

ACCESS ROAD: Paved

DIRECTIONS: From Santa Fe, travel north on US 285 to the town of Pojoaque, head west on NM 502 (in the direction of Los Alamos), and then proceed south on NM 4 to the monument. The route is clearly marked.

Frijoles Canyon Cliff Dwellings

Bandelier National Monument was named for the famed anthropologist and historian Adolph F. Bandelier, who came to New Mexico under the sponsorship of the Archaeological Institute of America in 1880. His fame stemmed from an ambitious goal to study the social customs, ancestral traditions, and lifestyles of the indigenous people of the Southwest by retracing their migration through the region. Bandelier explored a total of 166 ruins throughout New Mexico, Arizona, and Mexico in the course of his research.

Ten thousand years before Bandelier walked among the cottonwood trees at the base of Frijoles Canyon, ancient people migrated through the cool valley in search of wild game and plants for food. Due to their nomadic lifestyle, little remains from the ancient Paleo Indian and Archaic times to study. The oldest archaeological site found in Frijoles Canyon is an Archaic campsite thought to have been used in roughly 2010 B.C.

The Ancestral Puebloan (Anasazi) people are believed to have arrived in the area around A.D. 1100 and originally occupied pithouse communities scattered throughout the region. Like other ancestral cultures in the Southwest, the Anasazi became more and more dependent on crops like corn, squash, and beans for survival. The people gradually began to cluster together in large communities in order to share resources such as manpower, water, and cropland.

The Anasazi constructed large dwellings at the base of the towering cliffs and connected them to the natural caves that had been left behind by lava flows thousands of years before. These pueblo villages were built close to the bottom-lands along the creekbed where the ancient farmers planted crops and tended garden plots. The people also hunted small animals with snares and throwing sticks and pursued mule deer, bighorn sheep, black bears, and elk with bows and arrows. Ancient communities like those in Frijoles Canyon thrived because the residents adapted well to their environment.

Long House is a series of adjoining room blocks, 800 feet in length, that runs along the base of the sandstone cliffs overhanging the canyon. The multistoried, stone structures back up to a series of funnel-shaped caves—some excavated by hand and some carved by the natural forces of lava flow. These caves enhanced the space inside the pueblo structures, which were first inhabited in the 1300s.

Frijoles Canyon Cliff Dwellings

The ruins of **Tyuonyi** (pronounced chew-OHN-yee) rest on the canyon floor below the beautiful, towering cliffs. In its prime, this two-story circular structure contained as many as 400 rooms. Most of the daily activities in the village would have been conducted in the central plaza of Tyuonyi. The building may have also been used for defensive purposes, as the ground-level rooms had no exterior doors and could only be entered through hatchways in the roofs of some of the second-story rooms. The remains of three ceremonial kivas, adjacent to Tyuonyi, are also at the site. Tree-ring dating indicates that construction of this pueblo began more than 600 years ago, about the same time the caves of Long House were occupied.

Tsankawi, (pronounced sank-ah-WEE), an unexcavated pueblo, lies in the more remote second unit of Bandelier National Monument. Tsankawi was built in the 1400s and inhabited until the 1500s, and it included 350 rooms. This isolated pueblo sits high on a mesa, with breathtaking views of the steep canyons below. The trail to Tsankawi winds among huge boulders eroded by time. The sunsets from this remote site are well worth the 1.5-mile hike. Stop at the monument's visitor center for detailed directions to Tsankawi Ruins.

Other attractions to visit at Bandelier National Monument include **Kiva House, Ceremonial Cave, Painted Cave,** and **Frijoles Falls.** Access to the cave, off the Main Loop Trail, requires a 140-foot climb via four separate ladders, but is well worth the effort.

Tsankawi Ruins

55 JEMEZ STATE MONUMENT

P.O. Box 143
Jemez Springs, NM 87025
(505) 829-3530

NEAREST SUPPLY CENTER:
Jemez Springs, New Mexico

HIGHLIGHTS: Contemporary
Jemez people help visitors to
understand the importance
of this unique site, where an
early Jemez village and the
remains of a Spanish mission
stand side by side.

INTERPRETATION: Visitor center
and self-guided tours

SEASONS OPEN: All seasons

HOURS OF OPERATION:
8:30 a.m. to 5 p.m.;
closed Tuesday

FEE AREA: Yes

ACCESS ROAD: Paved

DIRECTIONS: Jemez State
Monument is in the historic
town of Jemez Springs,
which is 55 miles north of
Albuquerque and 30 miles
southwest of Los Alamos on
NM 4. The monument is
easy to find from the town
of Jemez Springs.

Jemez Pueblo and Mission

When Spanish conquistadors first arrived among the Jemez people in 1541, they were greeted by a group who had themselves migrated to the mountainous region. These natives, thought to be descendents of the Ancestral Puebloan (Anasazi) people, had moved south from the San Juan River area more than 500 years before in search of a new homeland and found the region around the Jemez River to be well suited to their agricultural lifestyle.

The Jemez people built and occupied several prosperous villages throughout the river drainage, and while some hamlets were closer to the water than others, all relied on the river for farming. The lush drainage and mountainous terrain also served to stock their storage rooms with wild plants and game including rabbits, mule deer, and bighorn sheep.

Giusewa, one of the original villages built by the Jemez, is the center of the ruins that make up Jemez State Monument today. It was on this village that Juan de Oñate focused much of his attention as he issued orders to Christianize the "savage" people. Converting the Indians in the Jemez River region proved to be a daunting task, for by that time the scattered villages housed more than 7,000 people. However, in 1621, native people were forced to leave their fields and build a magnificent mission that would one day bear the name San Jose de la Jemez.

Most of the archaeological excavations at Jemez State Monument have focused on the ruins of this huge church, which once stood 34 feet high and 131 feet in length. The walls of the church are 8 feet thick in some places and contained translucent sandstone windows which were quite innovative for the time. The magnificent structure's interior walls were decorated with beautiful frescos featuring religious themes, and one of the paintings has been refurbished and is on display.

Suit of armor of a Spanish conquistador, Albuquerque Museum

As their own sense of spirituality was cast aside, the native subjects of Giusewa became embittered toward the Spanish, and tensions escalated into a revolt. Spanish soldiers quickly suppressed the Indians, and 29 natives were executed in order to send a strong message about the consequences of defying Spanish rule. The revolt in Giusewa was not an isolated incident. Anger within the indigenous population was spreading across the Southwest, and the Spanish seemed oblivious to the seriousness of the conflict.

In 1680, the Jemez people joined the famed Pueblo Revolt. Much of the village of Giusewa was destroyed, but the Spanish were temporarily driven out of the territories of New Mexico. Unfortunately, the Spanish returned in full force 12 years later to regain power in the Southwest. As a part of this second conquest, the Jemez village of Astialakwa was attacked. Nearly 100 Indians were slaughtered and more than 300 were taken prisoner. Many of the native people fled the area and migrated north to live with the Navajo (Diné) in defensive pueblos in the Navajo homeland of Dinetah. Conditions along the Jemez River eventually improved, and the people slowly returned to the land they had farmed for generations. Contemporary Jemez people still consider this area and the ruins of Giusewa and Astialakwa to be sacred and important parts of their history.

56 CHACO CULTURE NATIONAL HISTORICAL PARK

P.O. Box 220
Nageezi, NM 87037-0220
(505) 786-7014

NEAREST SUPPLY CENTER:
Crown Point, New Mexico

HIGHLIGHTS: Chaco Culture National Historical Park is a place of mystery and intrigue for trained archaeologists and visitors alike. The prehistoric ruins along the wash at Chaco Canyon are some of the best-preserved and best-maintained sites in the United States.

INTERPRETATION: Visitor center, educational programs, self-guided and auto tours, and interpretive panels

SEASONS OPEN: All seasons

HOURS OF OPERATION: All hours (visitor center is open from 8 a.m. to 5 p.m.)

FEE AREA: Yes

ACCESS ROAD: Maintained gravel; some sections are impassable after heavy rains

DIRECTIONS: Chaco Culture National Historical Park sits in a remote section of northwestern New Mexico, between the towns of Cuba and Bloomfield and Cuba.

From the north: From US 550 (formerly NM 44), take County Road 7900, which is 3 miles east of Nageezi and approximately 50 miles west of Cuba. From the clearly marked turnoff, it is 21 miles to the park boundary. This includes 5 miles of paved road (CR 7900) and 16 miles of dirt road (CR 7950).

From the south: Reach CR 9 from either NM 605/509 or NM 371 (both originate from I-40) and proceed to the marked turnoff for NM 57/CR14. From here, 21 miles of rough gravel road will bring you to the visitor center. It is a good idea to call ahead if you are planning to come from the south, as these roads are impassable after heavy rains.

NOTE: Backcountry permits are required to access the more remote sites in Chaco Canyon. Permits and trail maps are available at the visitor center, and a loop road from the center leads to several easily accessible ruin sites as well as to the trailheads for the remote sites.

Chaco Canyon and Chaco Wash are known for blistering-hot summers, harsh winters, and short growing seasons made more challenging by the scarcity of water. However, it was within this severe environment that a very diverse and industrious prehistoric people built their sprawling communities and grew to influence cultures hundreds of miles away.

As you enter Chaco Culture National Historical Park, you are taking a huge step back in time. Nomadic bands of hunters and gatherers were the first to leave traces of their presence here roughly 8,000 years ago. As they roamed the semi-arid land, these people traded both goods and knowledge with other cultures in the region. Some experts believe that the early people of Chaco Canyon even traded with the farming people of Mesoamerica—a theory which explains how the Chacoan hunter-gatherers learned to plant corn.

Opposite: Pueblo del Arroyo

Pueblo Bonito

With the ability to cultivate a staple crop for food, the ancient people became more sedentary, inspiring a trend toward a more centralized society. As their culture advanced and farming increased, small pithouses were replaced by large pueblo-style dwellings. The thick stone walls now standing in ruins at Chaco Canyon reflect the final stage of this tremendous saga of social development, which began in roughly A.D. 920 and ended when the people drifted away from the canyon in small bands sometime after A.D. 1250.

The location of the communities at Chaco Canyon suggests that the area may have served as a ceremonial and economic trade center where prehistoric people living in the outlying communities came to participate in spiritual ceremonies and trade. The sophisticated road system that departs from the canyon was a direct and well-used travel route between the pueblos in Chaco and the remote communities to the north and south.

Thousands of ancient artifacts have been recovered over the years and, along with the ruins themselves, have helped to solve some of the mysteries surrounding the dynamic process of social growth in Chaco Canyon and the compelling influence of the Chacoans on the Ancestral Puebloan (Anasazi) people. However, the ruins visible in the canyon today are merely the tip of the iceberg. Hundreds and possibly thousands of structures remain buried beneath mounds of sand along the canyon floor. Some of these entombed structures were left covered by archaeological teams in order to save their contents for future study, possibly when more advanced methods can be used. Others were unearthed years ago, examined closely, and backfilled with sand to ensure their preservation.

Una Vida is the first site along the loop drive. This 150-room structure was built between A.D. 700 and 1100 and is believed to contain five ceremonial kivas, although it is mostly unexcavated. This site gives visitors a sense of how the ruins looked when archaeologists first came upon them. Look for a panel of petroglyphs close to this site.

Photos above: Pueblo del Arroyo

Pueblo Bonito

The building at **Chetro Ketl** was first constructed sometime around A.D. 1010 as a single-story structure and grew during its 30 years of use into a complex that covered nearly three acres. When it was completed, the D-shaped, two-story structure included as many as 16 kivas and more than 500 residential and storage rooms. Along with the visible walls exposed at Chetro Ketl there is a west wing that remains buried to preserve the artifacts for future discovery and research.

Pueblo del Arroyo contains more than 280 rooms and has an additional 20 ceremonial kivas. The pueblo was built in stages with the central section constructed sometime around A.D. 1075 and the north and south wings added between A.D. 1075 and 1105. Both the large, tri-walled structure on the west side of the pueblo and the central plaza are believed to have been added during the last phase of construction.

The skeletons of three macaws uncovered at Pueblo del Arroyo link the people here to those who lived in Mesoamerica—the birds' natural habitat. Macaws were treasured by the ancient people and treated as prized objects, and their bright feathers were used in ceremonial and religious purposes.

Kin Kletso is the next ruin along the road and is just a short hike from the west end of the loop road. It was believed to have been built in two stages, the first beginning around A.D. 1125 and the second around A.D. 1130. The pueblo's Great House contains over 100 rooms and may have risen to a level of three stories. Kin Kletso contains five enclosed kivas and was built during one of the last occupation periods at Chaco Canyon.

Casa Rinconada

The **Casa Rinconada** group is on the south side of the canyon and contains the largest known Great Kiva in Chaco Culture National Historical Park—about 63 feet in diameter. The short hike from the parking lot passes a number of smaller ruin sites believed to have served as residential units. Scholars estimate that there were as many as 300 of these residential rooms in the immediate vicinity of the Great Kiva at Casa Rinconada. The kiva, which was constructed during the last half of the 11th century, includes a ground-level entrance at one end and a very large antechamber and a number of smaller rooms at the other end. One of these smaller rooms is believed to have contained an altar that might have been used for private ceremonial rituals. The circular main chamber includes a bench that may have seated more than 100 people during ceremonies.

Experts wonder about the significance of this Great Kiva to the vast regions around Chaco Canyon. Could it have been a central gathering place for ceremonial rituals for the estimated 6,000 residents living within the far reaches of Chacoan dominion? Or is it just another construction masterpiece showing the architectural wisdom and expertise of these ancient people? Perhaps we will never know...

Pueblo Bonito

57 PUEBLITOS OF THE DINETAH

Bureau of Land Management
Farmington Field Office
1235 La Plata Highway
Farmington, NM 87401
(505) 599-8900

NEAREST SUPPLY CENTER:
Blanco, New Mexico

HIGHLIGHTS: The pueblitos, or small pueblos, in the Dinetah region are particularly intriguing to those with an adventurous spirit, as many of them are very remote.

INTERPRETATION: Information about the sites and private tour companies is available at the BLM field office in Farmington.

SEASONS OPEN: All seasons

HOURS OF OPERATION: All hours

FEE AREA: No

ACCESS ROAD: Gravel/dirt, often impassable after heavy rains. Be prepared to drive on unpaved roads for 60 to 80 miles both ways in order to reach the more remote pueblitos. High-clearance vehicles are recommended. Watch for heavy truck traffic due to mining in the area.

DIRECTIONS: The Pueblitos are scattered throughout the area around Largo and Gobernador Canyons, in northwestern New Mexico. Many of the sites in the region are just east of the small town of Blanco, which is on US 64, 22 miles east of Farmington.

NOTE: The Pueblitos of the Dinetah are managed by the Bureau of Land Management. Before you set off on your adventure, visit the BLM Field Office in Farmington for maps, directions, and tips on navigating the backcountry roads.

Many ancient Navajo legends and traditions originate from within the regions of Largo and Gobernador Canyons, and the Navajo people of today feel a great connection to the deep ravines and hillsides here. The Pueblitos in the Navajo homeland of the Dinetah are not just a scattered collection of ancient ruins dotting the landscape. They are testaments to the ingenuity and endurance of the Navajo people and reflect a brutal period of time when hostility and war were waged on the native populations of the Southwest by a variety of enemies, mainly the Spanish.

During the time period leading up to and after the Pueblo Revolt in 1680, some of the Navajo population moved into the remote reaches of Largo, Gobernador, and Crow Canyons, located south of present-day Navajo Reservoir. They welcomed the Ancestral Puebloan (Anasazi), and the two cultures lived in harmony in the Dinetah, blending their traditions and skills. Anasazi construction techniques soon replaced traditional Navajo architecture, and new and more complex masonry structures started to appear across the landscape of the Dinetah.

Life for the Puebloan and Navajo people was not easy, however. They lived in constant fear of their marauding enemies, including the Ute Indians, who raided farming communities throughout the Southwest. Between A.D. 1715 and 1750, the Navajo and Pueblo people built fortresslike pueblitos, perched on high bluffs, steep canyon walls, or in other areas where they could see for miles around. Sometimes the stone structures were even built atop huge boulders so that access to the quarters was virtually impossible without the aid of long ladders. Most of the pueblitos were constructed using unshaped sandstone slabs or blocks laid dry with little or no mortar, and many of the structures appear to have been built in haste. The pueblitos still standing today are the relics of a time of unrest.

By 1715, Ute attacks on the southern pueblitos of the Dinetah region were a common occurrence, which greatly distracted the people from their farming. This life of constant fear took its toll on the communities, and by the mid 1740s the pueblitos had been virtually abandoned.

Early Spanish settlers discovered the deserted structures, and archaeologists began documenting and excavating them in the early 1900s. In 1950, the Navajo Nation made a historic land claim in an effort to reclaim its ancient homeland, which brought about a complete documentation of the pueblitos in the Dinetah region. The BLM sponsored stabilization efforts at several of the sites, mostly in Crow Canyon, including **Canyon Petroglyphs, Crow Canyon Pueblo, Largo School Ruin, Hooded Fireplace Ruins, Tapacito Ruin**, and **Spit Rock Ruin.** Today, through the work of conservation groups and federal agencies, 48 sites in the Dinetah are listed on the National Register of Historic Places.

58 SALMON RUINS

6131 U.S. Highway 64
Broomfield, NM 87413
(505) 632-2013

NEAREST SUPPLY CENTER:
Bloomfield, New Mexico

HIGHLIGHTS: The pueblo
village now called Salmon
Ruins was occupied by two
separate groups of Anasazi
people, and the ruins reflect
the cultural differences of
these two populations.

INTERPRETATION: Museum,
visitor center, and self-
guided tours. Guided tours
are available with advance
reservations.

SEASONS OPEN: All seasons

HOURS OF OPERATION:
Weekdays, 8 a.m. to 5 p.m.;
Saturdays and Sundays,
9 a.m. to 5 p.m.; winter
Sundays from noon to 5 p.m.

FEE AREA: Yes

ACCESS ROAD: Paved

DIRECTIONS: Salmon Ruins
is on US 64, 2 miles west
of the town of Bloomfield.
The route to the ruins is
clearly marked from both
Bloomfield and Farmington.

The Ancestral Puebloans (Anasazi) who first built and occupied the Salmon Pueblo were attracted to the area by the rich soil and reliable water resources provided by the San Juan River, which flows close to the village site. Like the other farming villages along the San Juan River basin, the community at Salmon Pueblo relied on its agriculture.

The masonry walls at the site are believed to have been first constructed between A.D. 1088 and 1090 by Anasazi craftsmen. The distinct architectural style and thick stone walls of the pueblo are quite similar to those in Chaco Canyon, causing many scholars to believe Salmon Pueblo was one of the outlier communities of the thriving Chacoan culture.

The original, two-story pueblo dwelling included a back wall that extended from east to west and measured more than 130 meters in length. The ground floor contained more than 110 rooms while the second story added an additional 67. As is the case with other Chacoan outlier communities in the Southwest, the residential rooms and storage facilities at Salmon were built to face an open plaza with a Great Kiva. This keyhole-shaped kiva probably served as a ceremonial and community meeting place. A second kiva, also inside the physical walls of the pueblo, is now called Tower Kiva. Both of these structures convey a strong spiritual presence and suggest that the site may have been a spiritual gathering place for the greater Chacoan community.

For reasons unknown today, the Anasazi abandoned Salmon Pueblo sometime around A.D. 1130. The site stood empty until roughly 1225, when a second group of inhabitants arrived. The new occupants displayed cultural traits closely associated with the people of the Mesa Verde region in Colorado and may have migrated south after abandoning the cliff dwellings in what is now Mesa Verde National Park. These people made renovations to the pueblo that differed in architectural style from the original structures at the site, suggesting new attitudes toward building and use of space.

Tragically, during this second occupation, a raging fire broke out inside one of the rooms of the complex. The inferno spread rapidly and took the lives of many people including what archaeologists believe to be 30 to 50 young children. It is believed that the fire burned so intensely that it forged the sandy floor of the kiva into sheer glass. The famous Lizard Woman Fetish, now on display,

shattered in half during the blaze. After living at Salmon Pueblo for only 50 to 60 years, these people also abandoned the site.

The ruins are named for the Salmons, a pioneer family that homesteaded this area along the San Juan floodplain long after the departure of the ancient people. It was the foresight of this family that saved the stone structures from the greedy hands of collectors and looters who roamed the area. Thanks to the Salmons, the site is now under the stewardship and protection of the San Juan County Museum Association. The ruins belong to the people of San Juan County and are leased for public display. The facility relies heavily on donations, grants, and visitor fees.

59 AZTEC RUINS NATIONAL MONUMENT

84 County Rd. 2900
Aztec, NM 87410
(505) 334-6174

NEAREST SUPPLY CENTER:
Aztec, New Mexico

HIGHLIGHTS: This impressive
World Heritage Site was first
inhabited by Anasazi from
the Chaco Canyon region
and later by those from the
Mesa Verde area in Colorado.
The site includes a carefully
recreated Great Kiva.

INTERPRETATION: Visitor center,
museum, interpretive panels,
and self-guided tours

SEASONS OPEN: All seasons

HOURS OF OPERATION:
Summer, 8 a.m. to 6 p.m.;
winter, 8 a.m. to 5 p.m.

FEE AREA: Yes

ACCESS ROAD: Paved

DIRECTIONS: Aztec Ruins
National Monument is just
northwest of the town of
Aztec (about 14 miles north
of Farmington on NM 54).
Follow signs for Ruins Road,
on the north side of town,
which leads to the monument.

West Ruin

It is no wonder that the Ancestral Puebloans (Anasazi) chose to build their massive pueblo village at this beautiful site in the Animas River Valley. The river, fed by rainfall and snowmelt from high in the San Juan Mountains, provides a constant flow of water to the semi-arid land here, supporting diverse plant and animal life.

The walls that remain at the site today were constructed between A.D. 1110 and 1275 by the Chacoan people. Scholars believe the agricultural community here on the Animas River may have produced food for the growing Chacoan population living in the far-off boundaries of Chaco Canyon, more than 50 miles south. The crops were transported to Chaco Canyon along a road system that linked the communities at Aztec, Salmon, Casamero, and Chimney Rock to one another. In addition to food, commodities including timber, jewelry, pottery, and a host of other staples traveled along the connecting system of roads.

Sometime around A.D. 1150, the thriving community along the river began to suffer a steady decline, possibly due to drought, and the people eventually abandoned their village. Aztec Pueblo stood vacant until the early 1200s, at which time it was reoccupied. The new inhabitants had abandoned their cliff dwellings at Mesa Verde in Colorado and migrated southward in search of a new homeland. The Mesa Verde people lived in the ancient pueblo structures for several decades, and they refurbished many of the rooms and kivas during their occupancy. They also turned the rich soil of the Animas Basin into productive cropland once

Opposite: The Great Kiva

again. However, just as the Chacoans before them, the Mesa Verde people abandoned the site and migrated to the south and west of the San Juan Basin, leaving behind a treasure trove of artifacts that mark their short stay in the fertile valley.

The name Aztec is believed to have been applied by white settlers who first homesteaded northern New Mexico. The settlers associated the old pueblo structures they discovered with the stories they had heard about the Aztecs in Mexico; even though this assumption was mistaken, the name stuck. Sadly, these early settlers collected artifacts and dismantled some of the ancient structures to use the building material for their own homes. Looting and vandalism later plagued the ruins, too. Fortunately, archaeological enthusiasts came to the ruins' rescue, and the site was bought and protected by a series of private owners.

West Ruin

Excavation of the West Ruin began in 1916, followed by the Great Kiva and a number of smaller sites near the East Ruin. The massive East Ruin structure was found to include as many as 220 rooms on its ground floor, another 119 rooms on the second floor, and 12 third-story rooms. Like most Chacoan outlier communities, the Aztec Pueblo also contained numerous ceremonial kivas—29 including the Great Kiva. This impressive structure was rebuilt using the original excavation records as a blueprint, and the recreated kiva— the only one of its kind in the Southwest—gives visitors the opportunity to experience the remarkable ceremonial structure as it might have looked hundreds of years ago.

In 1923, President Warren G. Harding established Aztec Ruins National Monument. The site was placed on the National Register of Historic Places in 1966, and it joined the Chaco Culture National Historical Park as a World Heritage Site in 1987, an honor bestowed upon the facility by UNESCO (United Nations Educational, Scientific and Cultural Organization). While most of the artifacts recovered at the monument are now owned by The American Museum of Natural History in New York, a small collection of artifacts from the West Ruin are on display at the visitor center here.

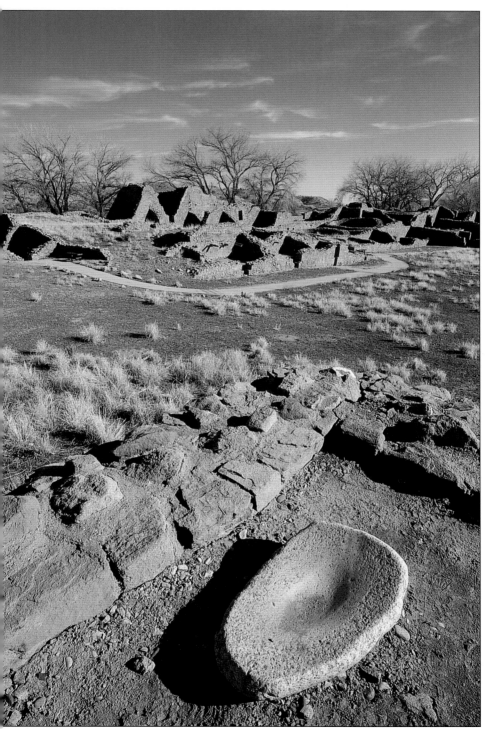

West Ruin

Mesa Verde National Park;
Right: Chimney Rock Archaeological Area

Colorado

Top: Lowry Pueblo;
Above: Anasazi Heritage Center;
Left: Ute Mountain Ute Tribal Park

60 CHIMNEY ROCK ARCHAEOLOGICAL AREA

P.O. Box 1662
Pagosa Springs, CO 81147
(970) 883-5359

NEAREST SUPPLY CENTER:
Pagosa Springs, Colorado

HIGHLIGHTS: The sites at and around Chimney Rock, and their mysterious relationship to those at Chaco Canyon in New Mexico, inspire the imagination and instill a deep respect for the people who first settled the Southwest.

INTERPRETATION: Visitor center and guided tours

SEASONS OPEN: May 15 through September 30

HOURS OF OPERATION: 9 a.m. to 4:30 p.m.

FEE AREA: Yes

ACCESS ROAD: Paved

DIRECTIONS: Chimney Rock is on CO 151, 3 miles south of its intersection with US 160. The site is east of Durango and west of Pagosa Springs.

Chimney Rock Pueblo

Chimney Rock and Companion Rock are rugged spires that reach like needles into the blue sky above the drainage of the Piedra River. The twin spires have served as points of demarcation for generations of travelers moving through the rugged area. The spires also stand guard over one of our nation's most intriguing archaeological sites.

Between A.D. 925 and 1050, the thick forests and mineral-rich banks of the Piedra River served as home for the Ancestral Puebloan (Anasazi) people. Long before the first European explorers set foot on the land, these ancient and industrious people utilized the resources they found in the dense forests along the Piedra River and dug pithouse dwellings in the rocky ground along its banks. They snared small animals living in the thick cover along the riverbanks and hunted large game such as mule deer, bighorn sheep, and elk in the forests around their encampments. The mountainous area also teemed with wild plants and herbs the people used for food and medicine.

Over time, cultivated crops became the mainstay of the Anasazi's diet, and the farmers diverted river water to irrigate their fields. They also built check

dams and soil-collecting systems to utilize water and soil resources, and constructed aqueducts to control spring snowmelt from the mountains and keep summer storms from flooding their crops. Some of these systems can still be seen at Chimney Rock. However, after generations of successful farming along the Piedra River basin, the ancient people started a slow but continuous upland migration. It is not clear why the people moved from the fertile, riparian areas, well suited to their agricultural lifestyle, to mountainous land virtually devoid of significant soil cover and water sources.

Once in the mountains, the Anasazi began building pueblo dwellings rather than the pithouses they had inhabited in the river basin. While this shift in architectural style was consistent with Puebloan communities throughout the Southwest, the buildings at Chimney Rock were often constructed in heavily wooded areas, which is relatively rare. The structures seen today were built during the latter stages of the site's development, sometime between A.D. 1000 and 1125, and display significant Chacoan influence, suggesting that the community here was closely associated with the people of Chaco Canyon in New Mexico.

The specific location of the famous Great House, or **Chimney Rock Pueblo** as it is known today, is believed to have been chosen for its proximity to the rock spires. Many believe the Anasazi centered their lives, planted their crops, and performed important ceremonies around a celestial calendar, and the Great House here supports that theory. During the period of lunar standstill, which happens every 18.9 years, the rising full moon is perfectly centered between the two rock spires. The fact that Chimney Rock Pueblo was built on a precarious ridge, accessible only by a narrow causeway, is also unique. Experts believe the ridge was

monitored from a structure at its far end in order to keep the pueblo safe from intruders. To archaeologists, the existence of this "guardhouse" suggests that the Great House was more than just a residential building, but its true purpose remains a mystery.

The elaborate pueblos that were built during this time period had exterior walls between three and five feet thick, and massive beams were required to support the imposing structures. Recent timber-source studies support the hypothesis that the village at Chimney Rock served as a major timber supplier for the pueblos of Chaco Canyon as well as its outlier communities. But how did the ancient people transport their timber to Chaco Canyon?

Chimney Rock Pueblo

"The Lumber Camp Theory" offers one explanation. Experts maintain that trees were harvested and dried along the forested slopes of the Piedra. Once winter snow accumulated, providing a slippery surface, the logs were slid down to the river basin where they sat until the raging spring runoff carried them downstream. The logs were floated from the Piedra River into the San Juan River until they reached Salmon Ruins, a Chacoan outlier community in present-day New Mexico. From there, porters may have carried the large beams to Chaco Canyon.

Photos above: Chimney Rock Pueblo

61 MESA VERDE NATIONAL PARK

P.O. Box 8
Mesa Verde National Park,
CO 81330
(970) 529-4465

NEAREST SUPPLY CENTERS:
Cortez or Mancos, Colorado

HIGHLIGHTS: Known for its Cliff
Palace, Mesa Verde National
Park's Ancestral Puebloan cliff
dwellings rank among the
country's foremost and best-
preserved archaeological sites.

INTERPRETATION: Museum,
visitor center, interpretive panels,
hiking trails, and ranger-guided
and self-guided tours

SEASONS/HOURS OF OPERATION:
Chapin Mesa Archaeological
Museum is open from 8 a.m.
to 6:30 p.m. from mid-April
to mid-October and closes
at 5 p.m. the rest of the year.
Far View Visitor Center is open
from 8 a.m. to 5 p.m. from
mid-April to mid-October.

FEE AREA: Yes

ACCESS ROAD: Paved

DIRECTIONS: The entrance to
the park is on US 160, 9 miles
east of Cortez and 35 miles
west of Durango. From the
park entrance, it is a 15-mile
drive to Mesa Verde's Far View
Visitor Center and 6 additional
miles to the park headquarters
and museum, located on
Chapin Mesa.

NOTE: The National Park Service
provides guided tours to some
of the ruin sites; registration is
at the Far View Visitor Center.
Hikers who wish to explore the
park must register at the chief
ranger's office, located near
the museum at Chapin Mesa.
The hiking trails in this area
are not difficult and present
wonderful overviews of the
canyon country.

Square Tower House Ruins

Mesa Verde National Park contains close
to 4,000 archaeological sites, and 600
of them are prehistoric cliff dwellings. The
archaeological record of this vast cultural and
historical resource led to its designation as a
World Heritage Site in 1978 by the distin-
guished World Heritage Convention of the
United Nations Educational, Scientific and
Cultural Organization (UNESCO).

Opposite: Cliff Palace

Kiva

Cliff House

Mesa Verde's impact on our present understanding of the prehistoric cultures that lived within the region is unmatched. Today, the archaeological treasures at Mesa Verde enable visitors to study well-preserved ruins, rock-art panels, and cliff dwellings, as well as to develop a much-needed sense of stewardship for this wonderful piece of our national heritage. The park is loaded with information about the ancient cultures of the Southwest, and it is committed to making important sites accessible to the public.

Experts believe that the first humans may have traveled through the deep canyons of Mesa Verde nearly 10,000 years ago, in the days when nomadic tribes roamed and hunted on the broad land now known as the Colorado Plateau. However, the earliest and most substantial evidence of continuous human occupation that has been found in the Mesa Verde area places the Ancestral Puebloan (Anasazi) people in the region around A.D. 550 to 750, during the Basketmaker era.

The inhabitants first lived in isolated villages on the mesatops overlooking the steep canyons. During the early stages of their social development, the Puebloan ancestors hunted wild game and gathered native plants, but their culture blossomed as they began to rely on domestic crops for food. The corn, beans, and squash the Anasazi cultivated thrived in the dry environment, fed by seasonal rains and rich soil.

The Anasazi built small farming villages that spread across the broad mesa landscape. At first, they lived in pithouses dug into the ground at a depth of 3 to 4 feet. Wooden pillars supported thatched roofs and thick adobe walls. Occupants entered the early pithouses through hatchways in the roofs and descended into the living spaces on wooden ladders. The same hatchways served as ventilation openings, allowing smoke from cooking and warming fires to escape. Some of the crude underground structures unearthed in Mesa Verde National Park contain circular or oblong living areas and smaller antechambers thought to have been used for storage.

As the Anasazi grew more accustomed to life on the high mesa, they developed more progressive agricultural methods. They used a system of holding reservoirs to collect water, which they diverted to their fields. A number of these prehistoric holding ponds have been uncovered at Mesa Verde, including the stone-lined dam found at Far View.

For reasons still unknown, around A.D. 1200 the farmers began to relocate from their mesatop villages to deep, cliffside alcoves, where they built large dwellings. The artfully constructed walls of the cliff dwellings at Mesa Verde were indeed the result of an unbelievable amount of physical labor and engineering. Large loads of building material were hauled up to the sites, which were accessed by climbing up sheer walls using footholds and handholds chiseled into the sandstone. It is almost unthinkable to consider scaling the walls of Mesa Verde burdened by a heavy basket filled to the brim with sandstone blocks. The workers also hauled water and dry clay, which they mixed to form the mortar used to secure the heavy building blocks in place.

Sadly, a severe drought between A.D. 1273 and 1285 gripped the land around Mesa Verde. This dramatic change in climate greatly challenged the people, who, by that time, had become almost completely dependent on their crops for survival. Scholars believe the huge quantity of food needed to sustain the large population at Mesa Verde, which may have peaked at 5,000, must have placed a good deal of stress on the communities along the canyon walls. The cliff dwellings were abandoned by A.D. 1300, and the people are believed to have migrated south into the land of the present-day Acoma and Pueblo tribes in New Mexico and Arizona.

For more than five centuries, the cliff dwellings of Mesa Verde lay silent until discovered by cowboys Richard Wetherill and Charlie Mason in 1888. William H. Jackson and Ernest Ingersoll, both members of the Photographic Division of the U.S. Geological and Geographical Survey of the Territories, later ventured into Mancos Canyon. It was Jackson's photographic work throughout the area that finally shed public light on the treasures of Mesa Verde, eventually leading to the preservation of many of the ancient ruins in this wonderful park.

62 UTE MOUNTAIN UTE TRIBAL PARK

P.O. Box 109
Towaoc, CO 81334
(970) 749-1452

NEAREST SUPPLY CENTER:
Cortez, Colorado

HIGHLIGHTS: A tour of the ruins at the Ute Mountain Ute Tribal Park provides a unique cultural experience and understanding of our country's ancient past.

INTERPRETATION: Access to the park is only granted if visitors are accompanied by a Ute tribal guide. Guided tours leave from the park's visitor center at 9 a.m. each day (check-in is at 8:30 a.m.)

SEASONS OPEN: All seasons (weather permitting)

HOURS OF OPERATION: Half-day tours run from 9 a.m. to 12:30 p.m.; full-day tours run from 9 a.m. to 4 p.m.

FEE AREA: Yes

ACCESS ROAD: Gravel

DIRECTIONS: The Ute Mountain Ute Tribal Park headquarters are at the intersection of US 160 and US 491 (formerly US 666), south of Cortez.

Tree House Ruins

The presence of the people who once filled the now-vacant cliff dwellings within the park seems to remain, surfacing as knowledgeable Ute guides share stories and facts passed down to them from their elders. Even though the Ute people claim no cultural ties to the ancient Ancestral Puebloan (Anasazi) people, they speak in reverence about the Old Ones who once roamed this land. In their view, all Native Americans owe their very existence to their connection to the land as well as their ability to hunt, gather, and grow the food they needed to survive. The Ute Mountain Ute Tribal Park is a 125,000-acre reserve set aside to preserve the ruins left behind by the Anasazi and to honor native culture, past and present.

The sites here are unique, for most of them appear as they were when first discovered by the Wetherill brothers in the latter part of the 19th century. The cliff dwellings were stabilized by the National Park Service in the 1970s, but pains were taken to ensure that the untouched character of the ruins remained intact.

The cliff dwellings along Johnson and Lion Canyons are thought to have been constructed by ancient people who originally lived in pithouse villages on the mesatops surrounding the deep canyons. According to tree-ring data gathered at several sites along Johnson Canyon, these people moved to the ledge sites and started to construct new dwellings sometime after A.D. 1130. The Anasazi continued their building efforts for about 30 years until the structures were deemed complete.

The dwellings remained as they were for another 30 years before a second stage of construction began. At the peak of their prosperity, the villages housed 200 to 250 people who hunted and farmed along the canyon floor and on the mesatops surrounding their homes. Archaeologists also believe the Anasazi who lived in the cliff dwellings here were closely associated with the Mesa Verde communities to the north and are thought to have actively traded with them.

The Ute Mountain Ute Tribal Park is a place where the serious archaeology buff and the amateur alike can come to understand the past in a very personal way. It is also a place where Native American people from throughout the Southwest, including the Hopi and Zuni, return to pray, hold ceremonies, and mingle with the spirits of their ancestors.

Morris Ruins

63 ANASAZI HERITAGE CENTER

27501 Highway 184
Dolores, CO 81323
(970) 882-5600

NEAREST SUPPLY CENTER:
Dolores, Colorado

HIGHLIGHTS: The center is a great introduction to the archaeology of the Four Corners area and provides visitors a sense of the history, cultural traditions, and social development of the Ancestral Puebloan people.

INTERPRETATION: Museum and interpretive panels

SEASONS OPEN: All seasons

HOURS OF OPERATION:
March–October, 9 a.m. to 5 p.m.; November–February, 9 a.m. to 4 p.m.

FEES: Yes

ACCESS ROAD: Paved

DIRECTIONS: The center is on CO 184, 3 miles west of the town of Dolores, and 18 miles north of the entrance to Mesa Verde National Park.

The Anasazi Heritage Center is operated by the Bureau of Land Management as a archaeological museum and helps preserve and display artifacts and records emerging from archaeological and anthropological research projects performed throughout the Four Corners area. It is estimated that the Anasazi Heritage Center stores and protects over three million artifacts and documents—a collection that grows substantially each year as scientific research continues throughout the Southwest. The center is the primary educational facility for the public on Anasazi, or Ancestral Puebloan, culture and their heritage.

The Anasazi Heritage Center was created as a result of one of the most extensive archaeological research projects ever initiated in the United States. In 1968, the federal government approved a plan to dam the Dolores River and construct McPhee Reservoir. In order to satisfy government requirements under environmental impact laws, however, a complete archaeological assessment had to be conducted before construction could begin. The assessment and study identified more than 1,600 archaeological sites and studied 120 of them extensively, uncovering a bonanza of artifacts that are on display at the Anasazi Heritage Center today.

The interactive exhibits at the center give visitors the hands-on experience of a true archaeologist. Microscopes are available for examining bone fragments, soil samples, and pottery shards that were uncovered during the Dolores archaeological project. Ancient tools, clothing, pottery, hunting implements, and replicated dwelling sites are also on display, accompanied by interpretive panels. The center maintains an extensive library and research laboratory to support its growing role in the protective care and analysis of artifacts from archaeological projects throughout the Southwest.

The Anasazi Heritage Center has two archaeological sites on its premises. **Escalante Pueblo** is on the hilltop above the museum and is accessed by a well-maintained path that begins at the parking lot. This site is believed to have been constructed in the early part of the 12th century. The 22-room pueblo was excavated and stabilized specifically to serve as an interpretive site for the public. The pueblo's style reflects that of New Mexico's Chaco Canyon, south of Dolores, causing experts to believe this village was a Chacoan outlier community.

Dominguez Pueblo, between the museum and the parking area, is a much smaller pueblo thought to have been the residence of a single family. When the site was excavated, the remains of a 35-year-old Anasazi woman were recovered. Her body had been entombed along with an assortment of artifacts including a turquoise frog pendant, a variety of ceramic vessels, and an assortment of bone tools. The gravesite also contained thousands of turquoise and shell beads, many of which were quite similar to those found at sites in Chaco Canyon. These beads provide another link between two ancient cultures separated by hundreds of miles.

Dominguez Ruins

We planned to spend only a day at the Anasazi Heritage Center, doing some research and looking at the exhibits before heading out to the sites in the Mesa Verde and Cortez area. However, we soon found ourselves surrounded by drawers full of artifacts and samples from sites throughout the Southwest, and our single day turned into several spent gathering information and building on our knowledge of the ancient Anasazi culture. The display of pottery, weapons, and household items at the center is a visual treat and helped us to get a clearer sense of the lives of the ancient people whose homes we photographed for this book.

It is difficult to conceive of a people who lived peacefully and harmoniously with nature, developed their own distinct architectural style, and grew crops on what seems to us like harsh, desert land. The climate on the mesa is one of extremes; scorching summer sun, high winds in the spring and fall, and harsh, cold winters. (Cathie and I first visited Mesa Verde after a good snowstorm, and we were amazed at how cold it was!) Yet the Anasazi people thrived in the cliff dwellings here for centuries.

Despite the rigors of farming, the people had time to make the beautiful pottery and other household items on display today at the Anasazi Heritage Center. These ancient relics give us glimpses of the rich and resourceful culture that called this region home, and help us to understand and visualize what life might have been like here thousand of years ago. For this reason, we both highly recommend a visit to the Anasazi Heritage Center before touring sites in the Cortez and Mesa Verde areas.

Dominguez Ruins

64 LOWRY PUEBLO

Anasazi Heritage Center
27501 Highway 184
Dolores, CO 81323
(970) 882-5600

NEAREST SUPPLY CENTER:
Pleasant View, Colorado

HIGHLIGHTS: This site, part
of Canyon of the Ancients
National Monument, is under
the stewardship of the Bureau
of Land Management's
Anasazi Heritage Center.
The pueblo and Great Kiva
here are examples of the
architectural skill and resource-
fulness of the Anasazi people
who called this place home.

INTERPRETATION:
Interpretive panels

SEASONS OPEN: All seasons

HOURS OF OPERATION:
All hours

FEE AREA: No

ACCESS ROAD: Partially paved
and well-maintained gravel

DIRECTIONS: Lowry Pueblo is
off US 491 (formerly US 666)
northwest of Cortez, 9 miles
west of the small town of
Pleasant View. The turnoff for
the site is on the outskirts of
town, and signs mark the way.

Great Kiva

As you look across the Great Sage Plain, it is hard to imagine that a very different landscape remains buried just a few feet below the ground. Beneath the sagebrush flats of Canyons of the Ancients National Monument, covered by windblown soil, rests one of the highest concentrations of archaeological sites ever found in North America. Lowry Pueblo, named for a local landowner, has been uncovered and is open for public view. The pueblo was excavated in 1930 by Dr. Paul S. Martin of Chicago's Field Museum of Natural History, and in 1967 the site was recognized as a National Historic Landmark. A number of stabilization projects have been successfully completed at the site and continue today.

Lowry Pueblo is believed to have been constructed from A.D. 1060 to 1150. However, the masonry pueblo that can be seen today covers a pithouse that was left behind by the ancestors of the Anasazi people. The reuse of building sites was common practice for the ancient people and is thought by some to be a sign of the overwhelming respect the Anasazi had for their land and their ancestors. The pueblo is thought to have been occupied for more than 160 years, starting as a small group of residential and storage rooms and containing a single, modest kiva. As time went on, the village grew in both physical size and number of inhabitants, and it was finally expanded into a large structure with as many as 40 rooms and eight ceremonial kivas.

The Great Kiva at Lowry is one of the largest that has been found in the area, measuring some 47 feet in diameter. Scholars believe the Great Kiva here probably indicates the social importance of Lowry Pueblo to the region as a whole. The village may have been a trade or ceremonial center for the substantial population of Anasazi people living throughout the Great Sage Plain.

Experts believe construction of the Great Kiva began around A.D. 1086, during the initial phase of building at the pueblo site. The kiva was spanned by a roof supported by four large beams that must have been carried to the site from the surrounding forest. The people probably entered the kiva through a hatchway in the roof or possibly through the smaller rooms to the north of the subterranean structure. The Great Kiva is still considered a place of reverence for contemporary native people.

Archaeologists have uncovered artifacts that link the Lowry Pueblo community to those in Chaco Canyon, to the south in New Mexico. The pueblo's layout and the masonry used in its construction, as well that of the Great Kiva, also reflect these Chacoan influences. Archaeologists wonder if Lowry Pueblo could represent one of the northernmost Chacoan outlier communities, despite the significant distance that separates these two ancient villages.

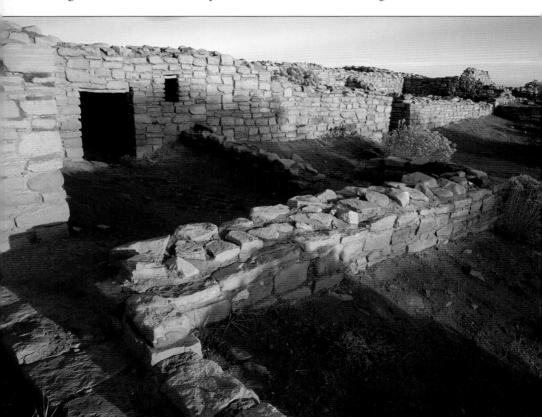

It was eleven o'clock when the flashes of lightning started to light up the Colorado sky above the ancient kivas and ruins at Lowry Pueblo. I watched for 15 minutes as I talked to Cathie on the cell phone. Other business had forced her to return to Montana for a bit, and we were planning her return.

As we were talking, the lightning moved closer to the ruins—and closer to the campground where our trailer was parked and where I was standing. I watched the spears of light strike the ground and was beginning to feel uneasy when Cathie said something that caught me completely by surprise. She is usually the more careful member of our team, and shock (luckily, not the electric kind) swept over me when she instructed me to get off the phone, set up my metal tripod and metal camera on the edge of the Great Kiva at Lowry, and do some time exposures while the heavy lightning approached.

I dutifully (and a bit skeptically) followed her directions, but after a dozen or so bright bolts of lightning I lost my confidence, folded things up, and dismissed my partner's artistic expectations as I hustled back to cover. But Cathie's intuition was correct! The images I managed to expose that night turned out to be awesome—charged with the high intensity of the natural world juxtaposed against the silent ruins. I couldn't help but wonder what the ancient people would have thought of this colossal light show from the heavens.

Suggested Loop Trips

During our many trips through the Southwest, Cathie and I have discovered several routes that are particularly enjoyable. We found that traveling these routes helped us minimize our driving time and expenses while giving us plenty of time to explore the ruins and rock-art sites. We've outlined five of our favorites for you here. You'll find the sites in bold, with accompanying page numbers so that you can flip to each entry for more information.

These loops vary in length, and your trip time will depend on the pace at which you like to go, the amount of time you spend at each site, and how often you stop to explore other aspects of the Southwest along the way. That part is up to you! As you may notice from the maps, you can link many of the suggested trips together for a longer adventure. (Indeed, there is a bit of overlap between some of the loops.)

The mileages we provide are all approximations (as we've found maps, odometers, and, yes, even guidebooks differ from time to time), but they should give you a good place to start. We recommend purchasing a set of maps before you take off on your journey, so you'll have another source to consult if navigating gets tricky. The "Recreational Maps" for each of the Four Corners states, published by GTR Mapping, are some of our favorites and are available where books and maps are sold.

Sego Canyon Rock-Art Site, Utah

Opposite: Canyonlands National Park, Utah

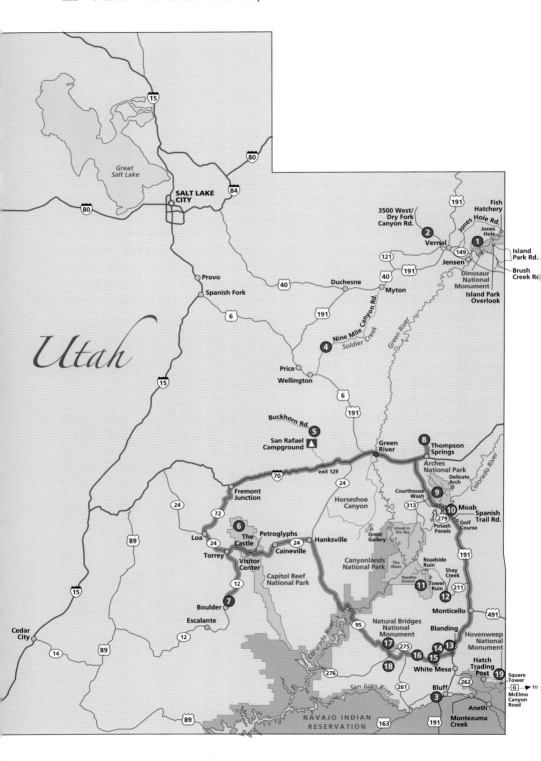

TRIP 1: **Green River Loop**

This loop, which begins in Green River, Utah, is roughly 600 miles when driven in its entirety (detours to sites off the beaten path included). It encompasses the sites in Utah's breathtaking canyon country, so the stretches between the ruins and rock-art sites promise to deliver spectacular scenery!

From I-70 in Green River, head east for 25 miles to the Thompson Springs Exit and continue north for 4 miles to the **Sego Canyon Rock-Art Site** (#8, p. 44) on the left side of the road.

Backtrack to I-70 and head west to its intersection with US 191. Go south for 21 miles to the intersection with UT 313. UT 313 will bring you to the northern entrance to **Canyonlands National Park** (#11, p. 55). Follow this road to the park's Island in the Sky Visitor Center. **Arches National Park** (#9, p. 47) is 5 miles farther south on US 191, just before the town of Moab and the **Moab Rock-Art Sites** (#10, p. 51). Once you've explored these areas, continue south for 40 miles on US 191 to UT 211, which leads to **Newspaper Rock** (#12, p. 60) and sites in the Needles District of **Canyonlands National Park** (#11, p. 55).

Return to US 191 and travel south about 36 miles to Blanding and **Edge of the Cedars State Park** (#13, p. 63). After enjoying the park, continue south for 4 miles on US 191 to UT 95 and head west. You'll see signs for **Butler Wash Ruins** (#15, p. 67), **Cave Tower Ruins** (#14, p. 64), **Mule Canyon Ruins** (#16, p. 69), and the **Grand Gulch Primitive Area** (#18, p. 76) along the way to **Natural Bridges National Monument** (#17, p. 73), about 35 miles from Blanding.

Continue on UT 95 until it intersects with UT 24, which you'll take west for roughly 40 miles to **Capitol Reef National Park** (#6, p. 39). From here, continue west on UT 24 to Torrey, where you can take a small 36-mile detour on UT 12 south to **Anasazi State Park** (#7, p. 42)—worth the trip!

Backtrack to Torrey and continue west on UT 24 for 15 miles to Loa, where a right onto UT 72 will lead you across the mountains for 36 scenic miles back to I-70. If you're still up for a bit of adventure on your way back to Green River, proceed north at Exit 129 for 27 miles on a well-maintained gravel road to the **Buckhorn Wash Rock-Art Site** (#5, p. 36).

Petroglyph, Capitol Reef National Park, Utah

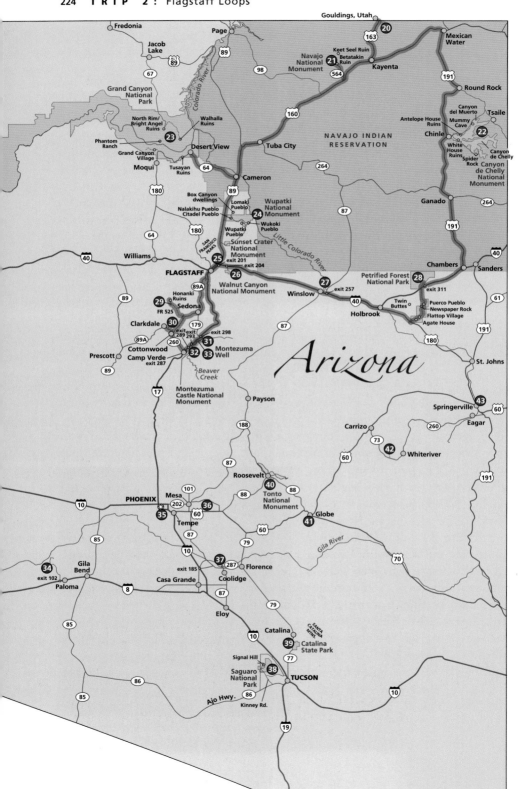

TRIP 2: **Flagstaff Loops**

This trip is two loops—one large and one small—that cover a great deal of ground in northern Arizona and pass through the amazing wilds of the Navajo Reservation. The large loop, northeast of Flagstaff, is roughly 650 miles; the "mini loop," just south of town, is about 125 miles. You can do them both together or choose the one that best fits with your interests and schedule. These loops can also be linked with Trip 3, the Phoenix Loop, for a full-scale road trip!

From Flagstaff take US 89 north for 1.8 miles to **Elden Pueblo** (#25, p. 105), on the left side of the road. Continue north on US 89 for about 35 miles to **Wupatki National Monument** (#24, p. 99), and then head north again, keeping an eye out for AZ 64, on the left. This highway takes you on a quick detour to **Grand Canyon National Park** (#23, p. 95), roughly 57 miles to the west.

When you're through taking in the grandeur, backtrack to US 89 and travel north again for 17 miles. When you reach US 160, follow it northeast for about 55 miles until you see signs for AZ 564, which leads 9 miles north to **Navajo National Monument** (#21, p. 89). Return to US 160 and continue northeast to Kayenta, where you'll find US 163, which leads north for 23 miles to **Monument Valley Navajo Tribal Park** (#20, p. 85). Return to Kayenta and continue northeast on US 160. Just after the town of Mexican Water, take US 191 south for about 60 miles to Chinle and follow signs to **Canyon de Chelly National Monument** (#22, p. 91). Return to US 191 and continue south for roughly 75 miles until it intersects with I-40 at the town of Chambers.

Take I-40 west toward Holbrook, and look for signs marking **Petrified Forest National Park** (#28, p. 111) at Exit 311. Follow the road south through the park, and head west when you reach US 180, which leads back to I-40 again. Head west on I-40 for 32 miles to Winslow, and follow signs to **Homol'ovi Ruins State Park** (#27, p. 109). Continue west, toward Flagstaff, for roughly 50 miles to Exit 204 and **Walnut Canyon National Monument** (#26, p. 107).

Once back in Flagstaff, you can add the "mini loop" to the trip by heading south on AZ 89A and continuing for 7 miles past Sedona. A quick detour north on FR 525 will take you to **Palatki Cultural Heritage Site and Honanki Ruins** (#29, p. 117). Back on AZ 89A, continue southwest through Cottonwood, then northwest to Clarkdale, and watch for signs for **Tuzigoot National Monument** (#30, p. 120). Backtrack from Clarkdale to Cottonwood, and take AZ 260 southeast to Camp Verde, where you can start heading north again, on I-17. At Exit 289, follow signs to **Montezuma Castle National Monument** (#32, p. 124), where you can get directions to **Montezuma Well** (#33, p. 126).

Once you're back on I-17 and heading north again, watch for the intersection with AZ 179 to Sedona. Turn right at that exit and travel south for 3.5 miles to the **V-Bar-V Ranch Petroglyph Site** (#31, p. 122). When you've finished touring the site, head back to I-17 and continue north to Flagstaff, completing the loop.

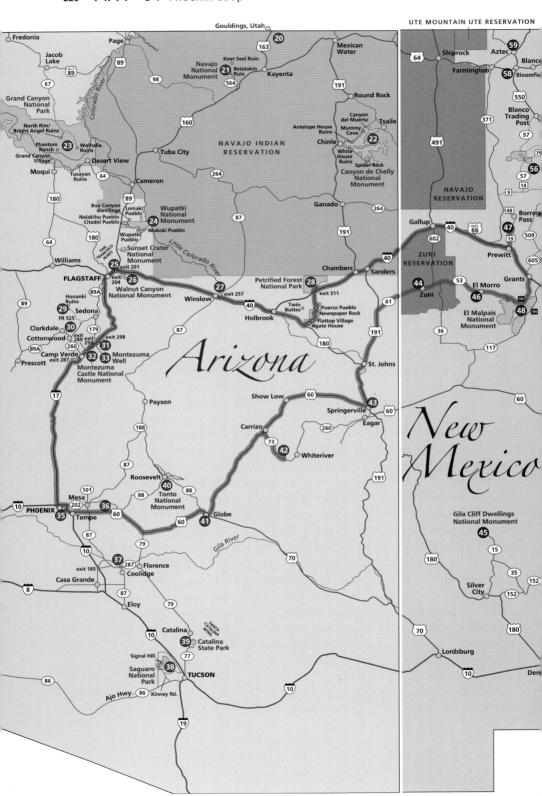

TRIP 3: **Phoenix Loop**

This trip through southeastern Arizona (with a brief stint in New Mexico) is roughly 775 miles in length. As we mentioned in the text for the Flagstaff Loop(s), Trips 2 and 3 can be linked for an even longer excursion. The sites along this loop range from remote backcountry stops to urban parks and full-scale monuments, so you'll get a taste of everything!

This loop begins at the **Pueblo Grande Museum and Archaeological Park** (#35, p. 130), located at 4619 E. Washington St. in Phoenix. From here, travel east on I-10 to Tempe, and take US 60 east to the town of Mesa and its historic **Park of the Canals** (#36, p. 132). Continue east to the Apache Junction exit, and proceed northeast on AZ 88 for 48 miles toward Roosevelt, following signs to **Tonto National Monument** (#40, p. 141).

After you've visited the monument, return to AZ 88 and follow it southeast for 29 miles to Globe and the ruins at **Besh-Ba-Gowah Archaeological Park** (#41, p. 143). Then head north on US 60 from Globe for roughly 57 miles to the town of Carrizo and the turnoff for AZ 73, which leads to **Kinishba Ruins** (#42, p. 147). When you are done exploring these ruins, return to AZ 73 and follow it through Whiteriver north to AZ 260. At the intersection with AZ 260, head east to Springerville and nearby **Casa Malpais Archaeological Park** (#43, p. 148). After you have toured the ruins, travel north from Springerville on US 191, pass St. Johns, and continue on US 191 until the intersection with AZ 61/NM 53, which heads east for 26 miles to Zuni, New Mexico, and the **Zuni Pueblo** (#44, p. 152).

Continue heading east on NM 53 for 30 miles to **El Morro National Monument** (#46, p. 157), then proceed for 16 more miles to the western trailhead of the **Zuni–Acoma Trail** (#48, p. 162). After you've explored the trail, continue on NM 53 (which bends to the north) to Grants and the intersection with I-40. Head west on the interstate for 19 miles to the Prewitt exit, and turn right on Historic Route 66 for a brief stint to County Road 19. **Casamero Pueblo** (#47, p. 161) is 4 miles north on CR 19.

Backtrack to I-40 and head west for roughly 145 miles through Gallup, New Mexico, and Sanders, Arizona, to Exit 311, where you will find the visitors center for **Petrified Forest National Park** (#28, p. 111). Travel south through the park for 22 miles to US 180 and head west for 19 miles to Holbrook and I-40. Take the interstate west toward Winslow, and watch for signs for AZ 87 and **Homol'ovi Ruins State Park** (#27, p. 109) at exit 257. After you've explored Homol'ovi, return to I-40 and continue west. Look for signs for **Walnut Canyon National Monument** (#26, p. 107) and Exit 204.

Head back to Flagstaff on I-40, then take I-17 south toward Camp Verde and look for the intersection for AZ 179 to Sedona in about 40 miles. Turn right at the intersection and then left, through the underpass, and go southeast (away from Sedona) for 3.5 miles to the **V-Bar-V Ranch Petroglyph Site** (#31, p. 122).

Return to I-17 and go south to Exit 289, where signs lead you to **Montezuma Castle National Monument** (#32, p. 124) and **Montezuma Well** (#33, p. 126). Go back to I-17 and it's a straight shot to Phoenix, 88 miles south.

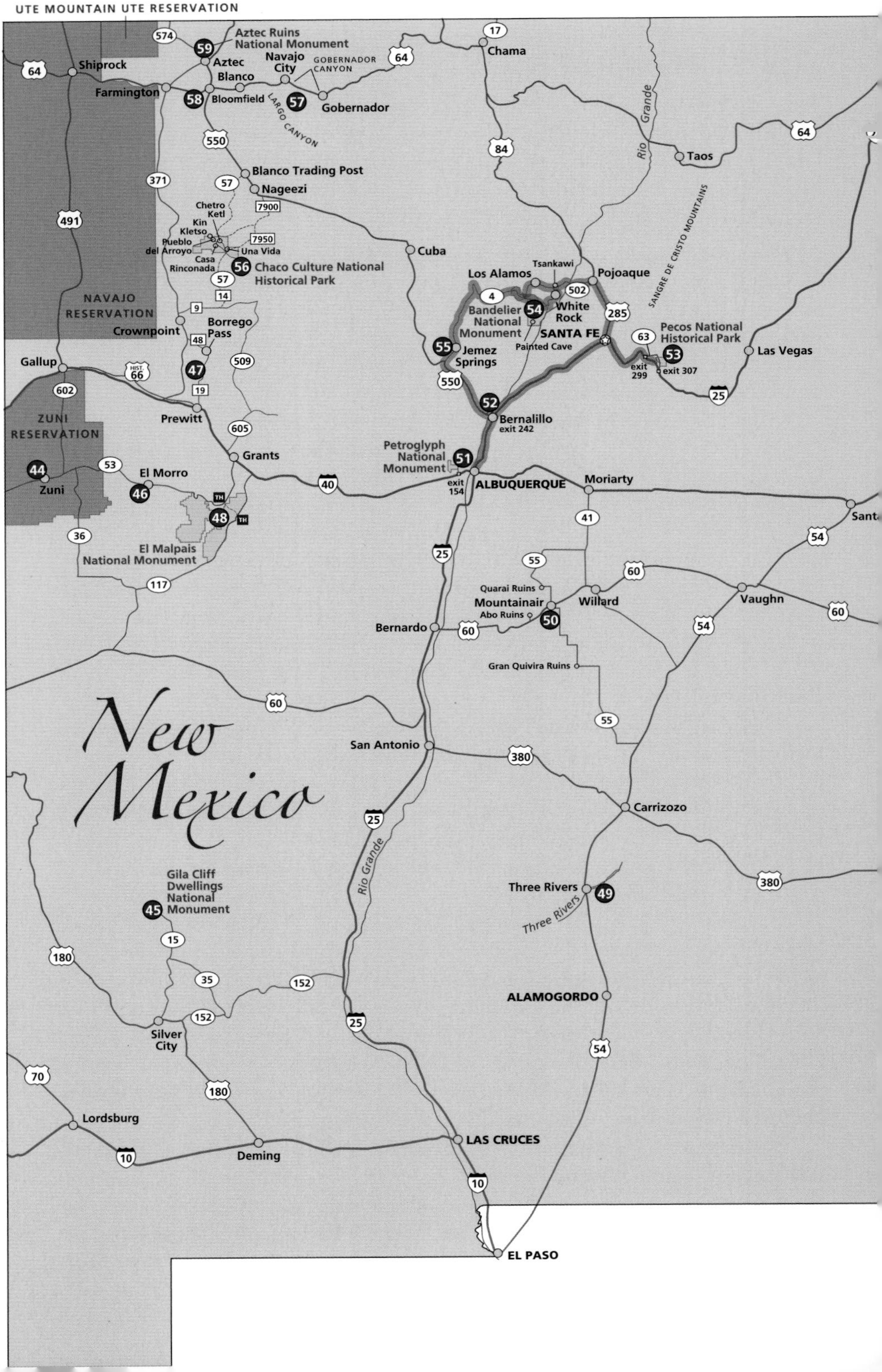
UTE MOUNTAIN UTE RESERVATION
Aztec Ruins National Monument
Shiprock
Aztec
Navajo City
GOBERNADOR CANYON
Chama
Blanco
Farmington
Bloomfield
LARGO CANYON
Gobernador
Rio Grande
Taos
Blanco Trading Post
Nageezi
Chetro Ketl
Kin Kletso
Pueblo del Arroyo
Una Vida
Casa Rinconada
Chaco Culture National Historical Park
Cuba
SANGRE DE CRISTO MOUNTAINS
Tsankawi
Los Alamos
Pojoaque
Bandelier National Monument
White Rock
NAVAJO RESERVATION
SANTA FE
Crownpoint
Borrego Pass
Painted Cave
Pecos National Historical Park
Jemez Springs
exit 299
exit 307
Las Vegas
Gallup
ZUNI RESERVATION
Prewitt
Bernalillo
exit 242
Petroglyph National Monument
Grants
El Morro
Zuni
exit 154
ALBUQUERQUE
Moriarty
Santa
El Malpais National Monument
Quarai Ruins
Mountainair
Abo Ruins
Willard
Vaughn
Bernardo
Gran Quivira Ruins
New Mexico
San Antonio
Carrizozo
Gila Cliff Dwellings National Monument
Three Rivers
ALAMOGORDO
Silver City
Lordsburg
Deming
LAS CRUCES
EL PASO

TRIP 4: **Albuquerque Loop**

This short loop—roughly 240 miles—is a perfect introduction to the ruins and rock art of the Southwest. The route links the cities of Albuquerque and Santa Fe, with a lot of breathtaking scenery and spectacular archaeological sites (some of them on little detours) along the way!

From the intersection of I-25 and I-40 in Albuquerque, head west on I-40 to Exit 154. Proceed north on Unser Boulevard for 3 miles to the entrance of **Petroglyph National Monument** (#51, p. 170). Then, backtrack to Albuquerque and head north on I-25 for about 65 miles (you'll pass the exit for Santa Fe) to the Glorieta-Pecos exit. From the small town of Pecos, follow signs to **Pecos National Historical Park** (#53, p. 175).

Backtrack toward Santa Fe on I-25, and proceed north on US 285 for 14 miles to the intersection with NM 502, which heads west for 19 miles to Los Alamos and nearby **Bandelier National Monument** (#54, p. 179), 11 miles south of town on NM 4. Signs for the monument are posted at the intersection of NM 502 and NM 4.

After you've visited Bandelier, travel west on NM 4 for 40 miles to Jemez Springs, the site of **Jemez State Monument** (#55, p. 182), and then follow NM 4 to the south until it intersects with US 550. Turn left and proceed southeast for 25 miles to **Coronado State Monument** (#52, p. 172); look for signs leading to the park. From here, continue southeast to Bernalillo and take I-25 south back to Albuquerque.

Pecos Pueblo and Mission Ruins, Pecos National Monument, New Mexico

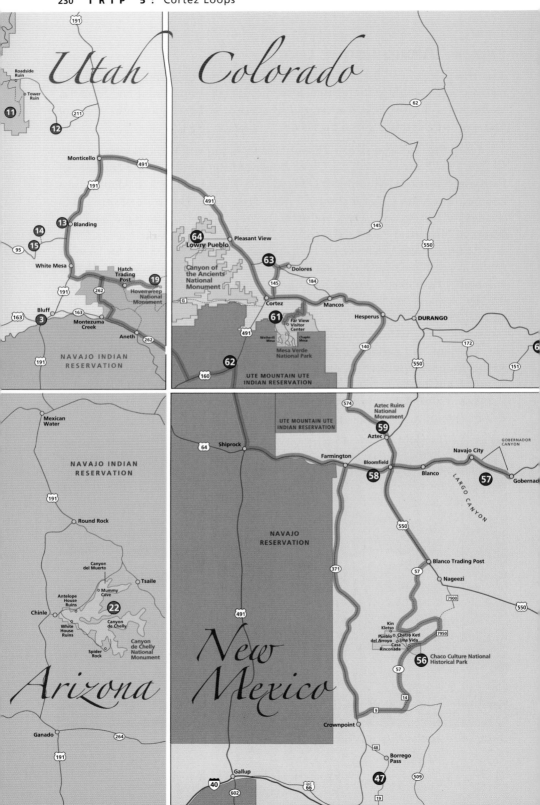

TRIP 5: **Cortez Loops**

This trip through the Four Corners region is composed of two loops, which together equal roughly 520 miles. The upper loop is about 340 miles and begins in Cortez, Colorado, and the lower loop drops down into New Mexico's San Juan Basin to visit Chaco Culture National Historical Park—a loop of about 180 miles. If you take a small detour to Four Corners National Monument, just off US 160 west, you'll be able to say you were in four states at once!

From Cortez, take CO 145 north toward Dolores and the **Anasazi Heritage Center** (#63, p. 214). Signs will guide you to the center, which is roughly 11 miles from the intersection of CO 145 and US 160. Backtrack to US 160, and head east for about 8 miles to the entrance to **Mesa Verde National Park** (#61, p. 207), then continue heading east on US 160 through Mancos and on toward Durango. When US 160 intersects with CO 140 (in roughly 25 miles), take CO 140 south to La Plata, New Mexico, and then head southeast on NM 574 to the town of Aztec and **Aztec Ruins National Monument** (#59, p. 197). From Aztec, follow US 550 south until it intersects with US 64 in Bloomfield. Proceed west on US 64 and watch for signs for **Salmon Ruins** (#58, p. 194), just west of Bloomfield.

Continue heading west on US 64 to Farmington and stop at the Farmington Field Office of the Bureau of Land Management to ask for directions to **Pueblitos of the Dinetah** (#57, p. 192), which are scattered throughout this region.

From Farmington, enthusiastic drivers can make a second loop in order to visit the sites in **Chaco Culture National Historical Park** (#56, p. 185). Though this detour adds about 180 miles to the route, the park is well worth the trip. Proceed back to Bloomfield and travel south on US 550 toward Nageezi. At the Blanco Trading Post, head southwest on NM 57, following signs to Chaco Culture National Historical Park. Continue on NM 57 through the park (it turns into County Road 14) to the intersection with County Road 9, then head west to NM 371, which will bring you north and back to Farmington in about 80 miles.

From Farmington, take US 64 west to Shiprock, then head north on US 491 (formerly US 666) for 21 miles to its intersection with US 160. Here, you'll find the headquarters of the **Ute Mountain Ute Tribal Park** (#62, p. 212). Take US 160 to the west for roughly 13 miles to the intersection with CO 41/UT 262, and proceed northwest. Keep your eyes peeled for signs directing you to **Hovenweep National Monument** (#19, p. 77).

Return to UT 262 and continue traveling northwest to its intersection with US 191. From here, head due north for 15 miles to Blanding and **Edge of the Cedars State Park** (#13, p. 63), then continue north for 21 miles to Monticello. From here, head southeast on US 491 for 40 miles to Pleasant View, and watch for signs to **Lowry Pueblo** (#64, p. 217). When you're done exploring at Lowry, continue heading southeast on US 491 to Cortez and the end of the loop.

Websites

UTAH

1. **Dinosaur National Monument:** nps.gov/dino
2. **Dry Fork Canyon Rock-Art Site:** blm.gov/utah/vernal/rec/dryfork.html
3. **Sand Island Petroglyph Site:** blm.gov/utah/monticello/
4. **Nine Mile Canyon Petroglyphs:** blm.gov/utah/price/9mile.htm
6. **Capitol Reef National Park:** nps.gov/care/
7. **Anasazi State Park:** stateparks.utah.gov/park_pages/anasazi.htm
8. **Sego Canyon Rock-Art Site:** blm.gov/utah/moab/
9. **Arches National Park:** nps.gov/arch/
10. **Moab Rock-Art Sites:** discovermoab.com/rockart.htm
11. **Canyonlands National Park:** nps.gov/cany/
13. **Edge of the Cedars State Park:** stateparks.utah.gov/park_pages/edge.htm
14. **Cave Tower Ruins:** blm.gov/utah/monticello/
15. **Butler Wash Ruins:** blm.gov/utah/monticello/
16. **Mule Canyon Ruins:** blm.gov/utah/monticello/
17. **Natural Bridges National Monument:** nps.gov/nabr/
18. **Grand Gulch Primitive Area:** blm.gov/utah/monticello/
19. **Hovenweep National Monument:** nps.gov/hove/

Salinas Pueblo Missions National Monument, New Mexico

ARIZONA

20. **Monument Valley Navajo Tribal Park:**
navajonationparks.org/monumentvalley.htm

21. **Navajo National Monument:** nps.gov/nava/

22. **Canyon de Chelly National Monument:** nps.gov/cach/

23. **Grand Canyon National Park:** nps.gov/grca/

24. **Wupatki National Monument:** nps.gov/wupa/

25. **Elden Pueblo:** fs.fed.us/r3/coconino/recreation/peaks/elden-pueblo.shtml

26. **Walnut Canyon National Monument:** nps.gov/waca/

27. **Homol'ovi Ruins State Park:** pr.state.az.us/parkhtml/homolovi.html

28. **Petrified Forest National Park:** nps.gov/pefo/

29. **Palatki Cultural Heritage Site/Honanki Ruins:**
fs.fed.us/r3/coconino/recreation/red_rock/palatki-ruins.shtml
fs.fed.us/r3/coconino/recreation/red_rock/honanki-ruins.shtml

30. **Tuzigoot National Monument:** nps.gov/tuzi/

31. **V-Bar-V Ranch Petroglyph Site:** rockart.esmartweb.com/vbarv/main.html

32. **Montezuma Castle National Monument:** nps.gov/moca/

33. **Montezuma Well:** nps.gov/moca/well.htm

34. **Painted Rocks Petroglyph Site:** phoenix.az.blm.gov/paint.htm

35. **Pueblo Grande Museum and Archaeological Park:** pueblogrande.org/

36. **Park of the Canals:** ci.mesa.az.us/parksrec/Parks/park_of_canals.asp

37. **Casa Grande Ruins National Monument:** nps.gov/cagr/

38. **Saguaro National Park West:** nps.gov/sagu/

39. **Romero Ruins:** pr.state.az.us/Parks/parkhtml/catalina.html

40. **Tonto National Monument:** nps.gov/tont/

42. **Kinishba Ruins:** wmat.us/wmaculture.shtml

NEW MEXICO

44. Zuni Pueblo: experiencezuni.com/

45. Gila Cliff Dwellings National Monument: nps.gov/gicl/

46. El Morro National Monument: nps.gov/elmo/

49. Three Rivers Petroglyph Site:
nm.blm.gov/recreation/las_cruces/three_rivers.htm

50. Salinas Pueblo Missions National Monument: nps.gov/sapu/

51. Petroglyph National Monument: nps.gov/petr/

52. Coronado State Monument:
nmmonuments.org/about.php?_instid=CORO

53. Pecos National Historical Park: nps.gov/peco/

54. Bandelier National Monument: nps.gov/band/

55. Jemez State Monument: nmmonuments.org/about.php?_instid=JEME

56. Chaco Culture National Historical Park: nps.gov/chcu/

58. Salmon Ruins: salmonruins.com/

59. Aztec Ruins National Monument: nps.gov/azru/

COLORADO

60. Chimney Rock Archaeological Area: chimneyrockco.org/

61. Mesa Verde National Park: nps.gov/meve/

62. Ute Mountain Ute Tribal Park: utemountainute.com/tribalpark.htm

63. Anasazi Heritage Center: co.blm.gov/ahc/index.htm

64. Lowry Pueblo: co.blm.gov/ahc/lowry.htm

Dry Fork Canyon Rock-Art Site, Utah   *Opposite: Mule Canyon Ruins, Utah*

Index

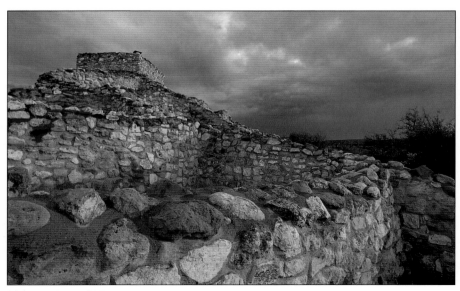

Tuzigoot National Monument, Arizona

About the Authors and Photographers

Gordon and Cathie Sullivan are blessed to live in the shadow of the majestic Cabinet Mountains, in the northwest corner of Montana. A short walk from their back door in Libby finds them in the depths of one of our nation's most rugged and remote wilderness environments, and a short drive finds them in Glacier National Park, a place they both love. From their home in the vast Rocky Mountains, the pair travels extensively throughout the West, and they have put together a collection of photographs that numbers in the hundreds of thousands, spanning the fields of historic, landscape, and wildlife photography.

The Sullivans' photographic work in the deserts of the Southwest was fueled by an intense interest in indigenous cultures and their closeness to the land. This project spanned four years and took them to hundreds of cultural destinations in the Four Corners region.

Gordon and Cathie have also collaborated on a number of photographic books including *Washington Impressions, Montana,* and *Gordon Sullivan's Glacier,* and their work has been published by *Audubon,* BrownTrout, CEDCO, Impact, and Willow Creek.